DEREGULATION AND LIBERALISATION OF THE AIRLINE INDUSTRY

Deregulation and Liberalisation of the Airline Industry

Asia, Europe, North America and Oceania

DIPENDRA SINHA
Department of Economics
Macquarie University, Australia

Ashgate

Aldershot • Burlington USA • Singapore • Sydney

© Dipendra Sinha 2001

Published by
Ashgate Publishing Limited
Gower House
Croft Road
Aldershot
Hampshire GU11 3HR
England

Ashgate Publishing Company
131 Main Street
Burlington, VT 05401-5600 USA

Ashgate website: http://www.ashgate.com

British Library Cataloguing in Publication Data
Sinha, Dipendra
    Deregulation and liberalisation of the airline industry
    Asia, Europe, North America and Oceania
    1.Airlines - Deregulation
    I.Title
    387.7'1

Library of Congress Control Number: 2001089072

ISBN 1 84014 835 7

Printed in Great Britain by
Antony Rowe Ltd, Chippenham, Wiltshire

Contents

List of Figures   *vi*
List of Tables   *viii*
Preface and Acknowledgements   *ix*

1.	An Overview of the World Airline Industry	1
2.	Airline Deregulation in Asian Countries	12
3.	Airline Deregulation in Australia and New Zealand	34
4.	Airline Regulation and Deregulation in Canada	53
5.	Regulation and Liberalisation of Airlines in Europe	67
6.	Evolution of Regulation and Deregulation of Airlines in the US	80
7.	The Theory of Contestable Markets and US Airline Deregulation: A Survey	103
8.	Effects of Airline Deregulation in the US	121

Bibliography   *149*
Index   *162*

List of Figures

Figure 2.1   Number of Domestic and International Air
              Passengers in India, 1970-98   14
Figure 2.2   Number of Domestic and International Air
              Passengers in Indonesia, 1970-98   22
Figure 2.3   Number of Domestic and International Air
              Passengers in Japan, 1970-98   25
Figure 2.4   Number of Domestic and International Air
              Passengers in Malaysia,1970-98   28
Figure 2.5   Number of Domestic and International Air
              Passengers in South Korea, 1970-98   30
Figure 2.6   Number of Domestic and International Air
              Passengers in Thailand, 1970-98   32
Figure 3.1   Business, Economy and Discount Airfare
              Indexes from the Fourth Quarter of 1992 to
              the Second Quarter of 2000   45
Figure 4.1   Growth of Real GDP, Air Passenger
              Kilometres and Population, 1961-98   54
Figure 4.2   Index Numbers of Employees in the Economy,
              Transportation and Air Transportation, 1961-98   54
Figure 4.3   Number of Domestic, Transborder and
              International Passengers (in thousands), 1980-98   61
Figure 4.4   Average Salary of Employees in the Airline
              Industry, 1961-97   62
Figure 4.5   Index of Productivity of Employees in the
              Airline Industry, 1961-97   63
Figure 4.6   Labour Cost Share of Operating Cost in the
              Airline Industry, 1961-97   64
Figure 4.7   Fuel Efficiency Index of the Airline
              Industry, 1961-97   65
Figure 4.8   Load Factor for Major Air Carriers, 1980-98   65

Figure 5.1   Number of Domestic and International Air
              Passengers in the European Union, 1970-98   68
Figure 8.1   Fatal Accidents per Million Aircraft
              Miles, 1938-99   142
Figure 8.2   Passenger Fatalities Per Million
              Aircraft Miles, 1932-99   143

List of Tables

Table 1.1	World Air Traffic and its Growth	2
Table 1.2	Privatisation of Airlines	6
Table 1.3	Number of Airline Alliances, 1994-96	8
Table 3.1	Performance Indicators of Selected Airlines in Australia and the US	41
Table 3.2	Movements in Average and Economy Fares: September 1990 to December 1991	43
Table 3.3	Regression Results for Discount Fares	48
Table 5.1	Air Transport Liberalisation Packages	73
Table 6.1	Benefits and Costs of Project A	82
Table 7.1	Nonstop Markets in the Domestic US for Trunk and Local Service Carriers	104
Table 7.2	Equations Explaining Average Load Factors	108
Table 7.3	Ratio of 1983 Fares to 1976 Deflated Coach Fares by the Number of Carriers in 1983 for Omaha	114
Table 7.4	Regression Coefficients Explaining 1985 Yields on Non-stop City Pairs	117
Table 8.1	Number of and Traffic at FAA Large, Medium and Small Hubs, 1969-97	122
Table 8.2	Number of EAS Communities and the Carriers Serving Them	130
Table 8.3	Size Distribution of the Subsidised EAS Communities	131
Table 8.4	Countries Having 'Open-Skies' Treaties with the United States	134
Table 8.5	Phillips-Perron (PP) Unit Root Tests	146
Table 8.6	Multivariate and Bivariate Granger Block Causality Tests	147

Preface and Acknowledgements

I think that there was a need for a relatively comprehensive and up-to-date book on airline regulation and deregulation in various parts of the world. There is an enormous literature on regulation and deregulation of airlines. Of course, it is not only the economists that have contributed to the literature. Whenever possible, I have drawn on the research done by other social scientists as well. My aim has been to reach a broad spectrum of readers. I hope that I have succeeded in doing so. This book should appeal to both academicians and others outside academia – people who are interested in issues relating to airlines. A few edited volumes deal with airline deregulation in different parts of the world. These volumes are either dated or lack a consistent approach. Thus, I think that this book fills a void.

My own interest in the economics of transportation in general and airlines in particular goes back to my days at the University of Nebraska-Lincoln (1981-86) where I did my Ph.D. in Economics. My advisor, Professor John Richard Felton from whom I took four courses in industrial organization and transportation economics, kindled my interest. My doctoral dissertation under Professor Felton's supervision also dealt with airline deregulation in the US. Later, in 1991, I started teaching transportation economics at Macquarie University, Australia. I owe special thanks to Professor Felton. I thank my past and present undergraduate and graduate students in transportation economics – I had a number of engaging discussions with them.

Most of the material for this book is new. However, I have used materials from the following three published articles:

Sinha, D. (1986), 'The Theory of Contestable Markets and U.S. Airline Deregulation', *Logistics and Transportation Review*, vol. 22, pp. 405-19.

Sinha, D. (1999), 'Evolution of Economic Regulation and Deregulation of Airlines in the USA', *Journal of Transport History*, vol. 20, pp. 46-64.

Sinha, D. and Sinha, T. (1994), 'Effects of Airline Deregulation: The Case of Australia', *World Competition*, vol. 17, pp. 81-96.

I thank Professor William Waters, Editor, *Transportation Research Part E: Logistics and Transportation Review* and Professor John Armstrong, Editor, *Journal of Transport History* for allowing me to use materials from the articles. I use materials from the article from *World Competition*, which I co-authored with the kind permission of Kluwer Law International. I also thank Ms. Frances Goldstone, Assistant Desk Editor at Ashgate Publishing for correcting typographical errors and inconsistencies in the manuscript.

Finally, I dedicate this book to my mother, Pratima Sinha and my father, Dwijendra Narayan Sinha. They have always supported me in all my academic endeavours.

Dipendra Sinha
Sydney

Chapter 1

An Overview of the World Airline Industry

Introduction

Microeconomic reforms not only in the field of airline regulation but also in other fields have been experienced with a much greater pace since the late 1980s and 1990s not just in the developed countries but also in the developing countries. The economies of the former Soviet bloc have also not been immune to the changes. The question about the pace of reforms has long been debated. While some economists prefer quick and drastic changes, others prefer slow and gradual changes. In the field of airline regulation and deregulation, economists have often argued that the United States followed the policy of 'big-bang' by passing the Airline Deregulation Act in 1978. This is contrasted with what happened in Canada and the European Union. These countries are said to have followed a policy of gradualism.

This chapter will discuss a number of general issues, which are important in the context of airline regulation and deregulation. This is the only chapter in the book, which gives some emphasis on international air services. Other chapters will deal more with air services within a country.

World Air Traffic

There has been a tremendous growth in air passenger and cargo traffic during the last decade. Table 1.1 gives the number of passengers in millions and cargo in million metric tonnes for various parts of the world for 1999 and the percentage changes from 1998.

Deregulation and Liberalisation of the Airline Industry

Table 1.1 World Air Traffic and its Growth

Regions	Passengers (in millions)	% chg vs. 1998	Cargo (in mil. m. t.)	% chg vs. 1998
Africa	74.7	11.3	0.8	0.9
Asia/Pacific	455.8	5.0	15.4	12.9
Europe	912.0	5.8	11.9	4.9
Latin Am./Caribbean	112.7	-0.9	1.6	0.3
Middle East	62.0	6.4	2.4	3.9
North America	1386.3	3.9	28.7	4.0
Total	3003.5	4.7	60.8	6.2

Source: Anonymous (2000e), p. 89

It is clear from table 1.1 that North America is the most important region in terms of both the number of passengers and amount of cargo. The region accounted for about 46 percent of the total passengers. Similarly, it accounted for about 47 percent of total cargo. Africa and Asia/Pacific accounted for the highest increases in 1999 in passenger and cargo respectively compared with 1998. However, the total number of air passengers remains low in Africa. The top ten airlines and the top ten airports during 1999 in different categories in descending order were as follows. In terms of revenue passenger kilometres, these were United, American, Delta, Northwest, British Airways, Continental, Lufthansa, US Airways and Singapore. The top ten airports in terms of cargo were all in the United States – Atlanta, Chicago, Dallas/Fort Worth, Los Angeles, Phoenix, Detroit, Las Vegas, Oakland, Miami and Minneapolis/St. Paul. The same for the passengers were Atlanta, Chicago, Los Angeles, London, Dallas/Fort Worth, Tokyo, Frankfurt, Paris, San Francisco and Denver.

Just like any other transportation activities, airline services have all the characteristics of services that have to be distinguished from goods. Air transportation creates both time and place utilities. Place utility is created by moving goods and people from the places where they are to where they need to be moved. Time utility is created when goods and people arrive in time. Delays can lead to additional costs. Also, demand for air transportation is a derived demand in the sense that the demand for these services arises from the demand for goods and the demand for being in certain places.

Even though air transportation is a service, it is much more capital intensive in nature. Aircraft, equipment, maintenance hangers, ground staff etc involve a large sum of money which are normally raised through the issue of stocks or through loans. The on-going replacement of aircraft also adds to the expensive nature of the business. Airline business is labour intensive in nature. Computers may have replaced the need for some workers, but airlines still need pilots, flight attendants, mechanics, baggage handlers, cleaners, managers, cooks, security guards, gate agents and the like.

Generally speaking, passengers account for more revenue than cargo in every country. In this book, we concentrate on air passenger service. Passengers can be divided into two types: business passengers and holiday passengers.

Another feature of the airlines is the seasonal nature of the airline business. The seasonal nature of the airline industry means that airline revenues fluctuate throughout the year. Load factor is a measure of how full an aeroplane is. Holiday seasons are marked by a tremendous increase in the load factor. A break-even load factor is the "the percentage of the seats the airline has in service that it must sell at a given yield, or price level, to cover its costs" (Air Transport Association, 2000). Naturally, rising costs increase the break-even load factor whereas rising fares lower the break-even load factor.

In the US, the break-even load factor is about 65 percent. Most airlines operate close to the break-even load factor. The number of seats in an aeroplane is a crucial determinant of per unit cost. The 'no-frills' airlines such as now defunct Peoples Express in the US used to add as many seats as possible to an aircraft to maximise revenue since it offered very cheap fares. On the other hand, some other established reputed airlines prefer to have a larger business class section with plenty of leg room and larger seats.

Overbooking is a strategy used by many airlines. Overbooking is used because the airlines expect that some ticket holders are unlikely to show up because they have changed their plans. If overbooking is equal to the number of no-shows, there is no problem. However, if overbooking exceeds the number of no-shows, passengers may need to be bumped and compensated. Airlines carefully study the history of the flight segments before deciding on the extent of overbooking.

3

Deregulation of airfares in many countries means that those airlines are now able to change the airfares quite frequently. The yield or revenue management is the process of finding the right mix of fares for each flight (Air Transport Association, 2000). This is a complicated process. Obviously, the aim is to maximise revenue from each flight. The airline has to carefully assess the demand for the flight before deciding how much discounting it will allow. Too much discounting will fill up all the seats quickly and may deprive an airline of the passengers who book at the last minute and are willing to pay higher prices. On the other hand, too little discounting may lead to a low load factor and thus, lost revenue. In planning such discounts, an airline has to take into account its rivals' strategies.

As Bailey, Graham and Kaplan (1985) point out, there are three categories of airline costs, namely, overhead costs, flight costs and passenger costs. Flight costs and passenger costs vary with the number of flights and the number of passengers, respectively. Unit operating costs of the airlines are affected by a number of factors. These include input prices (such as cost of labour, fuel costs, airport charges), productivity and operational characteristics (Alamdari and Morrell, 1997). Operational characteristics include length of haul, passengers or cargo, schedule or charter service and so on. Other things being equal, higher the length of haul, lower is the unit cost (i.e., cost per kilometre). Productivity is measured by per unit of the input. So far as airline costs are concerned, labour costs generally account for 25 to 35 percent of the total operating costs.

Seven Freedoms and Cabotage

International air traffic is governed mostly by the Chicago Convention (i.e., Conference on the International Civil Aviation in Chicago in 1944). The Convention set the seven freedom categories. The First Freedom refers to the right of flying over another country without landing. The Second Freedom refers to the right of a technical stop in another country for refuelling or repairs. The Third Freedom refers to the right of taking on passengers or cargo in the airline's home country and to carry them to a destination in a different country. The Fourth Freedom is just the opposite of the Third Freedom. The Fifth Freedom refers to the right to take passengers or cargo from other countries and take them to a destination, which is not the airline's home country. The Sixth Freedom is the right to pick up passenger or cargo in a foreign country and to put down the traffic in another foreign country via the home country. The Seventh Freedom is the right to pick up passenger or cargo in a foreign country and to put down the traffic in another foreign country. The first two freedoms are routinely granted by most countries.

Another important right is cabotage where an airline of one country is allowed to operate flights entirely within another country. It is interesting to note that cabotage has not generally been allowed even after deregulation of air services in many countries even though foreign equity participation has been allowed in many cases.

Privatisation

In this section, we look at privatisation of national airlines. Airline deregulation has been accompanied by privatisation in many countries around the world. The national airlines of many countries started off as state airlines.

Good, Roller and Sickles (1995) provide a number of arguments why state ownership is not desirable. First, productive efficiency is unlikely to be achieved when ownership is in the hands of an entity, which does not have the lowest monitoring cost. Second, the experience of state ownership in many parts of the world shows that access to subsidy tends to dilute the perusal of the goal of achieving productive efficiency. Third, while the objective of the private companies is to maximise profit, the objectives of the state enterprises may be many-fold. These enterprises may seek to limit competition limit with other state enterprises. Thus, the lack of competition may reduce efficiency. State enterprises may also have the additional objective of providing employment. This tends to result in a higher employment level than is desirable from an efficiency point of view.

A list of major airlines that have been privatised along with their dates of start of privatisation are given in table 1.2.

Table 1.2 Privatisation of Airlines

Airline	Privatisation Date	Airline	Privatisation Date
Air Canada	October 1988	Lufthansa	September 1989
Austrian Airways	January 1987	Malaysian Airlines	October 1985
British Airways	February 1987	Air New Zealand	October 1989
Japan Airlines	February 1987	Singapore Airlines	November 1985
KLM	April 1986	Thai Airways	March 1992
Qantas	July 1995		

Source: Al-Jazzaf (1999)

It is interesting to note that there were no state airlines in the USA at any point in time. Many industrialised countries have privatised their national airlines. Many developing countries are following suit. Malaysia and Thailand have partially privatised their national airlines. Talks are underway in India for partial privatisation of the national airline – Air India. However, in many cases, privatisation does not mean that all the shares of the airlines are owned by private individuals and not by the government. For example, the major stakeholder in Malaysian Airlines is still the Malaysian government.

Al-Jazzaf (1999) examines the impact of privatisation on airline performance in ten countries. The impact of privatisation on the following six variables are studied: sales, net income, total assets, employment, capital expenditures and dividends. The study finds that net income, total assets and capital expenditures grew at a moderate rate after deregulation while sales grew quite rapidly. The increase in the median dividends is found to be not statistically significant. However, the initial period after privatisation is accompanied by administrative and financial restructuring costs (besides the increase in capital expenditure) and this tends to reduce profitability. Contrary to the popular belief, the study finds an increase in employment after privatisation.

Frequent Flier Programs

While airline deregulation tends to increase competition, frequent flier programs tend to increase brand loyalty. In a sense, this goes against promotion of competition. Those who join the frequent flier program of an airline earn points when they take flights on the airline or its subsidiaries and/or use credit cards issued by the airline or stay in hotels designated by the airline. These points can then be used to get free tickets, upgrades and in some cases, merchandise.

The alliances among the airlines for the frequent flier programs are often global in nature. The biggest such alliance is the Star Alliance initiated by the United Airlines. Many important airlines such as Singapore Airlines, Thai Airways, Cathay Pacific, Malaysian Airlines, All Nippon Airlines, Swiss Airlines and Austrian Airlines are part of the alliance. Data on the travel characteristics of the members of the frequent flier programs are often used by the airlines to obtain valuable information about the passengers. But, there is also a significant economic impact of the frequent flier programs. Frequent flier programs restrict competition by discouraging entry of the smaller operators and limiting the potential growth of the existing smaller operators. Greater the size of the alliances, higher is the adverse impacts on the smaller airlines. One of the reasons why both Ansett Airlines and Australian Airlines (which merged with Qantas in 1994) introduced frequent flier programs in 1991 was to drive Compass, the new airline, from the airline markets in Australia.

Airline Alliances

The alliances tend to foster global networks. Alliances among airlines have become an increasingly common feature among the various airlines in the world. The process of alliances started in 1990. The basic motivation behind alliances is to reap the benefits of consolidation in the absence of mergers, which are not allowed by most governments. These alliances can take many forms. These may involve joint fare determination, catering, baggage handling, flight scheduling, and frequent fliers. In some cases, it may also involve code-sharing where an airline can sell tickets for services to be provided by the partner's routes. These alliances can also be route specific or could be on a regional basis.

7

Table 1.3 looks at the growth of international alliances during the period 1994-96. The alliances are changing the character of competitiveness of the airline industry internationally. At last count, there were 579 bilateral partnerships involving the 220 main airlines. There are five major groupings at present. In addition, there are a host of bilateral joint-marketing deals. To some extent, the alliances have been undermined by deregulation, which has allowed mergers in some cases.

The first international take-over in Europe took place in 2000. The Belgian flag-carrier, Sabena was allowed to be taken over by SAir (which is the parent company of Swissair) by the European Union, Belgium and Switzerland. This merger could destabilise the Oneworld alliance of which British Airways and American Airlines are major partners (Anonymous, 2000a). Sabena has a separate bilateral alliance with American Airlines. SAir is a member of the European alliance named Qualiflyer alliance. Thus, American Airlines can now join Qualiflyer alliance. This will irritate British Airways. The proposed take-over of KLM by British Airways would mean that British Airways would be a part of the Wings alliance built around Northwest and KLM. But, such an event will make it more difficult for British Airways to continue to be a part of the Oneworld alliance.

Table 1.3 Number of Airline Alliances, 1994-96

Number of Alliances	1994	1995	1996
With Capacity Stakes	280	324	389
Without Capacity Stakes	58	58	62
Without Equity	222	266	327
Including Code Sharing	111	140	180
New Alliances	NA	50	71
Number of Airlines with Alliances	136	153	171

Source: Productivity Commission (Australia) (1997), p. 8

Oum and Taylor (1995) discuss a number of advantages of such global networks. First, the potential benefits to consumers are lower joint airfares and a better quality of service due to less waiting time for connecting flights, higher service frequency, lower possibility of lost luggage and the faster accumulation of frequent flier points. Second, from the carrier's point of view, such a network is likely to increase efficiency. These include joint use of ground facilities, pooling of storage and maintenance facilities, joint buying of aircraft and other inputs and a leaner route structure made possible by the consolidation of networks by linking hubs to hubs and the avoidance of duplicate routes. These can result in a substantial increase in profit. For example, KLM announced that its alliance with Northwest would add around $150 million in additional profit. Similarly, Lufthansa gained an additional profit of $175 million in 1996 from its alliances with other airlines (Shifrin, 1997). Third, there are advantages to the carriers if we take into account the institutional and regulatory factors. The local carrier of a country has more knowledge of the institutional and regulatory arrangements as well as of the consumer preferences. In most countries, outright take-over of the airline by a foreign airline company is not allowed. Thus, networking is the next best thing.

However, as Gourdin (1998) points out, there are several disadvantages of alliances. First, some commentators have argued that alliances do not lower airfares. In fact, they tend to increase airfares particularly for business passengers who are less sensitive to price changes. Alliance members may rationalise fares, routes and services and as a consequence, passengers may have fewer choices. Second, Shifrin (1997) argues that such alliances have led to less competitive services in important international markets. Third, passengers are often not fully informed that they have to change to planes, which do not belong to the airline of their first leg of journey. The service may not be as good as the first airline that they boarded and it may lead to complaints. Fourth, it takes time for alliances to smooth out the operational kinks. Baggage delivery problems, late connection and incompatibility of the computer systems take time to be sorted out – as a result, passengers suffer in the interim. Employees often are reluctant to accept the alliances at least initially giving rise to further problems.

From the airline's point of view, the cost of joining an alliance has to be carefully weighed against the benefits of joining an alliance. Latecomers to the alliances face financial cost such as higher prorates and other commercial arrangements that could be thought of as an endorsement fee. There are differences between smaller and larger airlines when it comes to alliances. Larger airlines can bargain while the smaller airlines are more of a 'price-taker'. Japan Airlines joined OneWorld alliance in 1999 after a lot of negotiations with American Airlines, which is one of the prominent members of the alliance. Lufthansa also tempted Japan Airlines to join alliance with it but was not successful. Austrian Airlines has recently left Swissair's Qualiflyer alliance to join the Star alliance. In doing so, Austrian Airlines incurred a cost of US $42 million – 40% of the costs were for information technology. As Feldman (2000) points out, the latecomers face higher costs while alliance leaders face hidden costs.

General Agreements on Trade in Services and Its Implications for Air Service

Goods have been under the purview of the General Agreement on Tariffs and Trade (GATT) for a long period of time. However, services had been exempt from the purview of the GATT. However, under the Uruguay Round, which started in 1986 and ended in 1993, a General Agreement on Trade in Services (GATS) was introduced. GATS is alternatively known as the Services Agreement. Thus, for the first time, services were brought within a multilateral framework of rules and principles just like under GATT.

However, air service is characterised by many bilateral and multilateral agreements making it difficult to introduce uniformity. Thus, GATS has partial coverage for air service – these include the activities that are not covered by international agreements. The airline industry was apprehensive about the possibility of introducing a dual system of regulation by GATS. It felt that it was possible that while some countries might be applying GATS regulations while other countries would be applying existing arrangements. It was also thought that the International Civil Aviation Organisation (ICAO), the UN organisation, is better suited as a regulatory body in the international context.

Of course, only international air services would come under the jurisdiction of the GATS. GATS identify four modes of supply of services internationally. In the context of airline service, these are the following:
(a) cross-border: example, international flights;
(b) consumption abroad: example, services offered abroad to a national tourist;

(c) presence of natural persons: example, services provided by airline technical staff stationed abroad;
(d) commercial presence: example, services provided by an airline sales office located not in the home market.

Smithies (1995) discusses the air services that are covered by GATS. These are covered in the *Annex on Air Transport Services*. The so-called 'hard rights' are excluded from the GATS in air transport. These include pricing, routes, capacity and traffic rights. The Agreement covers only the following services:

(a) Computer reservation system (CRS) services: These cover information about fare and fare rules, airline schedule and availability.
(b) Selling and marketing of air transport services: This item does not cover pricing or conditions of airline services. Rather, it covers market research, advertising and distribution.
(c) Aircraft maintenance and repair services: This aspect relates to maintenance on an aircraft or its part when the aircraft is withdrawn from service – thus, line maintenance is not covered here.

In the case of goods, the most important principle of GATT had been the Most Favoured Nation (MFN) treatment. In the context of the GATS in airline service, the MFN principle means that all foreign suppliers are to be treated equally. However, the application of the MFN principle is particularly difficult in the context of the international air service because there are numerous bilateral arrangements between many countries.

Smithies (1995) feels that the GATS in services will have little impact on international air service in the short run. However, the long run impact is not yet clear cut. The search for new regulatory arrangements got an immediate boost from the GATS. The Fourth ICAO Air Transport Conference held in November 1994 was a direct result of the GATS. It was urged at the conference that ICAO should take the leading role in developing economic regulation and in developing co-operation. Even though the trend towards free trade is well established for goods, it is not so clear-cut in the case of services. The modes of transportation are quite regulated.

It is possible that the scope of the GATS in international air service may be broadened in the future. It is likely that regional integration will play an important role as well.

11

Chapter 2

Airline Deregulation in Asian Countries

Introduction

The diverse Asia-Pacific region, according to International Civil Aviation Organization (ICAO), comprises of 34 nations and some dependent territories. Even though it includes Australia and New Zealand, we discuss the process of airline deregulation in Australia and New Zealand in a separate chapter. Also, we concentrate on a few countries in Asia, namely, India, Indonesia, Japan, Malaysia, South Korea and Thailand.

The share of scheduled international traffic in the Asia-Pacific region in the world has increased tremendously. According to Taneja (1988), a number of factors were responsible for this phenomenon. First, many of the Asian economies maintained a high rate of growth, which has been partially fuelled by increasing exports. Second, some Asian airlines, which have lower costs, were able to offer world class service. Third, there had been greater co-operation between the airlines and the home country governments. Fourth, the willingness on the part of many governments and airlines to follow pro-competitive policies had been a factor.

The importance of airline transportation in the Asia-Pacific region can be attributed to four important factors according to Taneja (1988). First, many countries in the region are islands or archipelago countries. Examples are Indonesia and the Philippines. Second, as pointed out earlier, the growth in international trade has necessitated more reliance on air transportation. Third, the Asia-Pacific region contains a very high percentage of the world's total population. Thus, even though the demand for air travel is, at present, relatively low due to the lower per capita income in many Asian countries, the potential for growth is enormous. Fourth, tourism is a major industry for many countries in the area and air travel is often the only way of arrival for tourists from other countries.

The demand for air service is increasing in the Asia/Pacific region at a faster rate than any other region in the world. According to the forecasts of the Air Transport Action Group, the share of the Asia-Pacific region in the world will increase to 42 percent in 2020 from 29.9 percent in 1995.

It is impossible to talk in general terms about the evolution of deregulation of airlines in Asia. While Europe also has many countries, the development of the European Union and to some extent, the common approach towards deregulation makes the task easier.

The recent recession in many Asian economies had hit the airlines hard. The yield (which is the price the average passenger pays to fly one mile or kilometre) for these airlines fell by ten percent between December 1997 and December 1998.

Regulation and Deregulation of Airlines in Selected Asian Countries

Next, we turn to regulation and deregulation of airlines in some Asian countries. Our choice of countries here is highly selective. The choice was dictated by the availability of information and interests of the author.

India

With a population second only to China and a burgeoning middle class, India is now on a steady growth path. After independence in 1947, India's goal of establishing a "socialistic pattern of society" was set by the first Prime Minister of India, Jawaharlal Nehru. India always had an active entrepreneurial class. However, over time the role of the government increased and many cumbersome rules and regulations restricted the activities of the private sector.

In 1969, the government nationalised the major banks. Bureaucracy and regulation hindered economic growth. Regulation benefited the government servants and the ministers more than anyone else. During the late 1970s and 1980s, India did make some attempts to free the private sector from the shackles of complex regulations. In 1991, India was on the verge of a foreign exchange crisis. The IMF was urging India to open up its economy and free itself from the unnecessary rules and regulations. A series of measures were undertaken to liberalise the economy. Some of these measures also related to the airline industry. A number of exciting developments have taken place since then. In fact, in some ways, India has greater potential than China (Sinha and Sinha, 1997).

Figure 2.1 shows the number of domestic and international air passengers in India. For a country of its size, India had a very modest number of air passengers in 1970. The number grew from 2.67 million in

13

1970 to about 11 million in 1992. After a decline, it increased to 16.5 million in 1998.

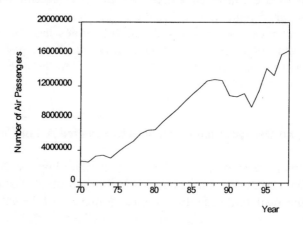

Figure 2.1 Number of Domestic and International Air Passengers in India, 1970-98
Source: World Bank (2000)

Until the early 1990s, the government of India had a virtual monopoly in the airline business in India. The domestic routes were served by Indian Airlines while the international routes and sometimes connecting domestic routes were served by Air India. Before independence, India had a fairly large number of private airlines. The most important of them was Tata Airlines was set up in 1932 by J.R.D. Tata who is called the 'Father of Indian Civil Aviation'. The airline was nationalised in 1953 and was re-named Air India. However, Tata remained the Chairman of Air India for the next 25 years and kept a tight control over Air India's affairs (Mhatre, 1999a). The result was that Air India retained the ethos of the private sector. In 1962, Air India became the world's first all-jet carrier with a fleet of six 707s. Similarly, a number of other airlines were nationalised and consolidated to form Indian Airlines.

The above structure remained unchanged till the 1970s. The schedules of Indian Airlines were limited in nature and many smaller cities were not well served. To provide feeder service, the government introduced Vayudoot in 1981. However, there were pressures from both inside and outside the country to open the air services to the private sector.

14

Until the end of the 1980s, the Air Corporations Act of 1953 governed the activities of the airline industry in India. Under this Act, only Indian Airlines and Air India, both government-owned airlines, were permitted to offer air services in the country. Naturally, the government was in charge of setting fares and routes to be served by these airlines. Air India was mainly in charge of providing international services and Indian Airlines was serving mainly domestic routes. Many unprofitable routes had to be served by Indian Airlines because it was under social obligation to do so.

In April 1990, the government adopted the open-skies policies. This policy allowed the entry of the air taxi operators (ATO) and ultimately, scheduled new entrants. The open skies policy was the handiwork of the then Civil Aviation Minister Arif Mohamed Khan. Lagging tourist traffic because of insufficient capacity and an enormous amount of uncleared export air cargo prompted the Minister to declare an open skies policy for charters (Mhatre 2000, p. 9). In addition, the air taxi operators were now allowed to provide scheduled services. The idea goes back to 1986 when the then civil aviation minister Jagdish Tyler tried to introduce it. However, restrictions on the size of aircraft and departure times prevented the scheme to be operational at that time.

In 1991, the government of India announced a number of measures aimed at liberalising the maze of licensing and other types of control of the economy. For a discussion of the consequences of liberalisation of the Indian economy, see Sinha and Sinha (1994b). India also liberalised its airline markets and bilateral agreements with carriers were signed. Indian Airlines was restricted to its operations within India. However, in 1993, the Ministry of Civil Aviation allowed it to start its service to the Gulf countries as well. The 1993 Indian Airlines pilots strike was a watershed in the history of civil aviation in India. Private airlines such as East West, Jet, Damania and Modiluft got tremendous boost from the vacuum created by the strike. East West was particularly successful – it was offering 8000 seats daily using 10 737s by mid 1994. However, a number of airlines, such as Air Asiatic, Continental Air Link and UB Air collapsed because of the huge debts that they piled up. In 1993, Vayudoot, which had accumulated losses of $60 million, was merged into Indian Airlines and Indian Airlines hired all its staff of 1,800.

In 1994, the Department of Civil Aviation set out the conditions for those ATOs seeking to provide schedule services. Six ATOs were given permits to operate scheduled services in October 1994.

15

In another important development in March 1994, the Air Corporations Act of 1953 was repealed. This changed the way in which Air India and Indian Airlines were governed. Both airlines, which used to be government enterprises, were now changed to limited liability companies. With this change, domestic companies, Indian nationals and foreign companies could become part owners of both Air India and Indian Airlines. This cleared the deck for eventual privatisation of Air India and Indian Airlines which is yet to take place. Other regulatory changes were also made. Overseas corporate bodies are now allowed to establish Indian companies to provide air taxi services. 100 percent equity participation is allowed in such cases. However, there are restrictions on repatriation of investments and dividends. Domestic airlines have now been allowed up to 40 percent foreign equity participation.

The Kelkar Committee was set up in 1997 to recommend measures to increase the efficiency of the government owned domestic airline: Indian Airlines. The Committee had the task of finding ways to infuse capital into Indian Airlines. The Committee recommended that the government should reduce its holding to 49 percent, Indian Airlines employees should hold 10.6 percent and the remaining 40.4 percent should be with the public. The government accepted the recommendations of the Kelkar Committee but no action has been taken so far.

The government owned Indian Airlines still has the bulk of the share of the total domestic air traffic. Indian Airlines has been suffering losses partially due to the opening up of the market. In May 1999, the government of India announced that Air India would be partially privatised. For a number of years, the carrier has been plagued by mismanagement and high costs. Government of India has also announced that shares of Indian Airlines would also be floated in the open market paving the way for the partial privatisation of the airline. However, it has not yet materialised even by the end of October 2000. The government has also approved plans to corporatise five major airports: Bangalore, Calcutta, Chennai, Delhi and Mumbai (previous name, Bombay). The government would allow 74 percent of the funds to come from foreign investment.

Even though, Indian Airlines has the dominant position in the domestic market, the growth has been slow. The other two major private carriers, Jet Airways and Sahara Airlines also compete aggressively in terms of fares and services. In 1987-88, the monopoly Indian Airlines carried 10.4 million passengers. In 1998-99, the three carriers, Indian Airlines, Jet Airways and Sahara Airlines carried 12 million passengers. Thus, in spite of the impressive growth of GDP during the last ten years, the growth in air passenger traffic has been slow.

There are a number of reasons for such slow growth. Unlike in many other countries, leisure traffic is still small and business travel accounts for over 90 percent of the passenger traffic. The liberalisation of the economy in the 1990s means that the businesspersons' needs to travel to Delhi and other major cities to seek licenses or permission for routine business work is now much less than before. Moreover, improvements in telecommunication and courier services and the introduction of electronic mail have also lessened the need for travel.

By the middle of 1990s, it was believed that India was poised for a higher growth of air service. Private airlines were making plans of huge expansion. Damania was planning to build a training base in Nasik in the state of Maharashtra. East West was setting up an inspection and repair unit. The new entrant NPEC also had a grand expansion plan. Ultimately, Damania, East West and NPEC all collapsed. The lack of professional management was one of the important reasons for the failure. Meanwhile, the Tata industrial group was proposing to set up an airline by tying up with Singapore Airlines to fill the void left by Damania, East West and NPEC which were then about to fail. The then Civil Aviation Minister C. M. Ibrahim opposed the proposal arguing that a foreign airline would not allowed to enter the domestic market. The Tata industrial group proposed an alternative plan of having institutional investors instead of Singapore Airlines. After three years of protracted negotiations between the Tata industrial group and the central government, the plan did not materialise. Meanwhile, in 1996, Indian Airlines created a new subsidiary, Alliance Airlines to provide feeder services using 737-200s. This was a part of the rationalisation plan of bringing the capacity in line with the demand in the non-major sectors.

Private operators are becoming important players in providing air services. These accounted for a little over 40 percent of domestic air traffic in 1998. The number of passengers carried by the private airlines increased from a mere 15,000 in 1990 to 4.9 millions in 1998 (Department of Economic Affairs, 2000).

Now, there are only two private airlines, namely, Jet Airways and Sahara Airlines, which are competing with Indian Airlines which is dogged by ageing fleet and financial problems. By the first half of 2000, the domestic market share of Indian Airlines slipped below 50 percent for the first time. Its share in October 2000 was about 46 percent.

Jet Airways expanded rapidly and its share of the domestic market grew to 35 percent in 1999. It made further gain during 2000 when the share of Indian Airlines fell. Its fleet size is currently about half of that of the Indian Airlines. Initially, Sahara was a minor player in the market. However, it is now set to expand. Sahara is a conglomerate with interests in finance, real estate, exports, consumer products and media (Mhatre, 1999b). 40 percent of Sahara is owned by the employees. Sahara accounted for about seven percent of the share of the domestic market in 1999. By 1999, it offered 3,300 seats daily with 28 flights to 14 destinations. Sahara has also experienced gain in traffic in 2000 but not by as much as Jet Airways. Sahara has set up an aviation academy, which offers courses in management, ticketing, traffic handling etc.

Restrictions on import by the airlines have also been eased. All scheduled airlines and air taxi operators no longer require import licenses to import new aircraft. Also, they need not pay import duties.

However, a number of controls still remain. At present, the regulatory and developmental functions of civil aviation are looked after by the Ministry of Civil Aviation and the Directorate General of Civil Aviation (Department of Economic Affairs, 1998). The Directorate General of Civil Aviation still has controls over routes that are served by the scheduled airlines and the aircraft they import. Private carriers are not yet on a level playing field. Private scheduled carriers face restrictions on the types of aircraft that they can import and operate. They can only import and operate Boeing 737s and turboprop aircraft. They are required to provide feeder services without any subsidies. Loss making services cannot be abandoned by the airlines. Infrastructure facilities provided to the private airlines are still inadequate and less than what is provided to Air India and Indian Airlines. The state still has control over aviation fuel price – airlines pay almost the double the world price.

In the United States, airline deregulation led to the development of a hub and spoke system. Existing regulations in India do not permit the development of such a system. This affects the profitability of the airlines.

Air India and Indian Airlines are also plagued by the fragmented nature of the labour organisations representing airline staff – there are as many as 18 of these organisations.

Even though the two state-owned airlines have advantages over the private airlines, especially in the availability of infrastructure facilities, the effect of the open skies policy on them has not been positive. Competition can deliver more benefits only if the players are given equal opportunity in responding to changes in market conditions. However, the state airlines are still under government controls, which prevent them from responding adequately to these changes (Mhatre, 2000). Indian Airlines was adversely affected by the introduction of the private carriers because now it had to share the major profitable trunk routes with the private carriers. Moreover, it lost a large number of skilled personnel who moved to the private carriers because of the much higher salaries and benefits. Both Indian Airlines and Air India are still beset with financial problems. Indian Airlines along with its subsidiary Alliance Air is struggling to maintain the number of passengers. Its fleet has remained the same during the last decade.

Air India is faring no better. Its fleet has virtually remained the same. Air India has withdrawn services from many of its routes especially from those serving Europe. It is now planning increasingly to have code-sharing arrangements with the foreign carriers that serve cities in India. For example, it entered a code-sharing arrangement with Virgin Atlantic Airways in December 1999. By the arrangement, Air India gave three of its unused quota of flights per week between India and London to Virgin Atlantic. In return, Air India gets a block of eight upper class and 56 economy class tickets at a fixed rate. Air India is free to sell these tickets at a premium. Code-sharing arrangement is scheduled to be extended to the flights between India and New York, which are scheduled to be started by Virgin Atlantic. The CEO turnovers in both Air India and Indian Airlines have been quite rapid. The CEOs who did not tow the Ministry of Civil Aviation ministry line had to leave. Several CEOs who demanded more autonomy were given the sack.

At present only Air India and Indian Airlines are authorised to offer international services. The government is considering allowing private airlines to offer international services on a limited scale. According to the proposal, the private airlines will be allowed to offer such services only if national airlines refuse to serve the routes.

Earlier, there were two separate bodies, namely, International Airport Authority of India (IAAI) and National Airport Authority (NAA) which were in charge of providing infrastructure facilities in international and national airports respectively. The enactment of the Airport Authority Act, 1994 created a single body called Airport Authority of India (AAI) in April 1995. AAI made an after tax profit of 2080 million rupees in 1998-99 as against a profit of 1960 million rupees in 1997-98. Much of the increase can be attributed to airport charges and cargo income (Department of

Economic Affairs, 2000). Much remains to be done to reduce the traffic congestion in some major airports such as Mumbai.

Gallaghar and Jenkins (1996) note that the carriers in Mumbai had to operate under 15-minute separations. It was estimated that two-minute reduction had the potential of increasing traffic growth by one percent.

The government formulated a comprehensive policy on airport infrastructure in December 1997. The policy recognises the role of private sector (including foreign firms) which could bring more resources for the airports as well as lead to an increase in efficiency in management.

The International Airports Division (IAD) is in charge of management, operation and development of the five international airports.

An important development in the regulation of civil aviation in India is the Civil Aviation Act 2000, which is to be introduced by the end of 2000. The new act called Civil Aviation Act has the following goals:

(a) better development and regulation of civil aviation including operation of air transport services to meet the needs of the people for safe, secure, regular, efficient and economic air transport;

(b) establishment of the Civil Aviation Authority;

(c) continued adherence by India to the Chicago Convention, the Tokyo Convention, the Hague Convention and the Montreal Convention including Montreal Protocol;

(d) Adherence by India to the Convention for Unification of Certain Rules Relating to International Carriage by Air signed at Montreal on 28th May, 1999.

The proposed Civil Aviation will have the following functions:

(a) The functions conferred by licensing of air transport, licensing of aerodromes, regulation of air seat and air cargo capacity and the provision of information;

(b) The functions conferred with respect to registration of aircraft, airworthiness of aircraft, the safety of aircraft operations, the certification of operators of aircraft and licensing of air crew, air traffic controllers and aircraft maintenance engineers;

(c) functions relating to safeguarding civil aviation against unlawful interference; and

(d) such other functions as may be conferred on it by the Central Government from time to time.

(Ministry of Civil Aviation, India, 2000)

Estimation of Price and Income Elasticities   For developing countries, there are not many studies which estimate price and income elasticities for air service. For India, one such study is by Gallaghar and Jenkins (1996).

Gallaghar and Jenkins use International Civil Aviation Organization data to estimate the elasticities. The model used for deriving the estimates makes traffic growth a function of changes in population, changes in GDP and changes in airfares, which reflect the changes in unit costs which had been falling. As aircraft utilisation (as measured in hours a day) increases, unit costs fall. Aircraft utilisation is one way of measuring the productivity of the airline. Underutilisation can be due to various factors such as inefficient operating practices, poor infrastructure facilities, and low demand for airline service. However, government regulations can also cause low utilisation.

The study finds both price and income elasticities to be higher in India than in the developed countries in Western Europe and the US. The income elasticity is found to be in the range between 1.56 and 1.75 which is higher than the typical estimates for the developed countries. The price elasticity for the domestic trunk routes is found to range between 2.0 and 2.3, which again is higher than the typical estimates obtained in the developed countries. Thus, economic growth is found to be less important than the changes in fares in generating the growth of traffic.

The recent opening up of the skies has led to a pent-up demand and fare has been more of a driving force than even the growth of income. However, the growth of traffic in the major trunk routes might have been be hindered by the lack of capacity in the major airports. As noted earlier, traffic congestion at the major airports has been a problem.

Indonesia

With a population of 220 million, Indonesia is the fourth most populous country after China, India and the United States. It has 13,600 islands. Thus, air service is vital to Indonesia.

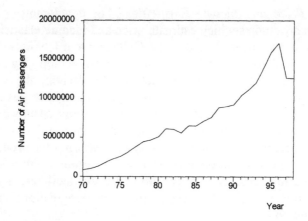

Figure 2.2 Number of Domestic and International Air Passengers in Indonesia, 1970-98
Source: World Bank (2000)

The Asian crisis and the currency collapse hit Indonesia hard. By the middle of 1998, domestic air services had been reduced by 40 percent and the load factor had plummeted to 30 percent (Thomas, 1998).

Unlike many other countries in the region, Indonesia had two airlines which both of which operate international routes as well. Garuda Indonesia is the flag carrier of Indonesia. Merpati Nusantara Airlines also operates international routes. Merpati used to be a subsidiary of Garuda Airlines. However, on 29 April 1997, the government delinked Merpati from Garuda. It is mostly a domestic airline – three of its 218 routes are international. Merpati was forced to buy domestically produced IPTN aircraft (which is produced by the government of Indonesia) which was of low quality. As a result, Merpati's costs were high because of the need to frequently change the spare parts. The Asian crisis hit Indonesia hard and the airlines were no exception, According to some analysts, from its humble beginning in 1962, Merpati has carved a niche. In 1996, its share of domestic traffic was 38 percent.

In addition to the two state-owned airlines, Garuda Airlines and Merpati Nusantara Airlines, there were three other privately owned smaller airlines. These are Buraq, Mandala and Dirgantara Air Service. However, in early 2000, seven new private carriers were given licenses to operate - these are Air Wagon International (AWAIR), Bayu Indonesia Air, Indonesian Airlines, Pelita Air Service, Lion Mentari Air (Lion Air), Jatayu

Air and Rusmindo Interusa Air. AWAIR is serving both domestic and international routes. It holds the licenses to operate 27 domestic routes and 28 international routes. The executives of the new airlines were confident that there were room for the new airlines because of the expected increase in demand. Moreover, the existing airlines had abandoned important routes as a part of consolidating their position. The new airlines proposed that they would initially operate on those routes, which were either not served or inadequately served by the existing airlines. Existing carriers have accused the new airlines of selling tickets far lower than market prices.

There was yet another airline in Indonesia. Sempati Airways which was partly owned by PT Humpass Group (a conglomerate controlled by Suharto's youngest son, Hutomo Mandala Putra) and the other part by the Indonesian Air Force (Bowen and Leinbach, 1996). Even though PT Humpass Group held 15 percent of Sempati's stock, Suharto's son controlled another 40 percent of the stock through a Malaysian company, Asean Aviation. Sempati's load factor had fallen to about 30 percent in 1998. It had cut ticket prices by 40 percent to attract more passengers. However, more than 85 percent of its costs were denominated in US dollars. The steep fall in Indonesian rupiah dealt a severe blow to the airline. The immediate cause of the collapse of Sempati in June 1998 was attributed to its inability to pay $5 million to the government-owned P.T. Pertamina oil company from which Sempati had bought fuel for credit. Of course, Suharto's fall and therefore, his inability to come to his son's rescue was also a cause of the failure of Sempati.

Garuda almost collapsed during the height of the Asian crisis in 1997. The fall of the currency, government intervention and falling traffic had severe impacts on the airline. Garuda still has a debt of $.18 billion which is to be restructured in a deal that has been agreed by the government.

In 2000, Garuda has turned around. It has once again become profitable after three years of reorganisation. It has been helped by Lufthansa Consulting in its bid to become more efficient. Garuda's route structure and fleet has been rationalised. Unprofitable domestic and international routes have been dropped. This has resulted in cutting services to ten domestic, two Middle Eastern and seven Asian routes. The passenger load factor has increased significantly to reach an average of 70 percent. Per seat revenues which had declined to 3.5 US cents in 1998 are now about 5.5 US cents (Anonymous, 2000c). The process of privatisation of Garuda is scheduled to begin in 2002.

Japan

The Allied Forces did not allow any commercial services within Japan during the first few years of its occupation. There are three dominant airlines in Japan and there are a number of regional subsidiaries of these carriers. These three airlines are Japan Airlines (JAL), All Nippon Airways (ANA) and Japan Air System (JAS). These three airlines account for 95 percent of the passengers carried by Japanese airlines.

Japan Airlines (JAL) was established as a private air carrier to serve domestic customers in 1952. In 1953, the government invested in half of the capital stock of the JAL and JAL became partly government owned. During the same year, Japan Airlines started its international services.

The domestic market of Japan is about one-tenth in terms of revenue passenger kilometres (RPKs) and one-sixth in terms of the number of passengers of the US airline market (Yamauchi and Ito, 1996). However, these numbers do not reflect the fact that the very fast and efficient train system is Japan is a very important substitute for the airlines.

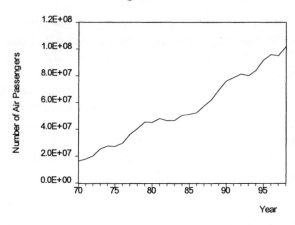

**Figure 2.3 Number of Domestic and International Air Passengers in
        Japan, 1970-98**
Source: World Bank (2000)

Figure 2.3 shows the number of domestic and international air
passengers in Japan for 1970-1998. The number of air passengers has
increased steadily and at a fast rate from 1.63 million in 1970 to 50.5
million in 1980 and then to more than 100 million in 1998.

One important feature of the Japanese airline system has been strict
regulations of the airlines. Just like what CAB did in the United States,
fares were regulated and set strictly on the basis of distance. Route density
was not taken into account even though it clearly affects the cost of
providing air service. Thus, fares bore little relationship to the cost of
production and cross subsidisation was rampant. Generally, such cross
subsidisation meant that the services on the trunk routes subsidised the
local routes. A number of changes and mergers have resulted in the present
three dominant airlines (JAL, ANA and JAS).

The so-called 'aviation constitution' was adopted in 1972. This
constitution laid down specific rules for the division of the Japanese
market. ANA was to serve domestic trunk routes, local routes and short-
distance international charter flights. JAL was to serve the domestic trunk
routes and the international routes. JAS was to serve local routes and some
of the domestic trunk routes. The markets were segmented in such a way
that there was hardly any competition in the domestic trunk routes and of
course, there was no competition in the international routes so far as

Japanese carriers are concerned. To that extent, the regulation was even stricter than in the case of CAB regulation in the US because CAB regulation did allow competition to a greater degree. The demand for air travel grew rapidly in Japan during the 1970s but the pressure for changes were mounting as well. The US airline deregulation, the Canadian experiment with liberalisation and the European move towards deregulation were adding to the pressures for changes in the system. However, changes were slow in coming.

At the request of the Minister of Transport, the Council for Transport Policy submitted its final report in June 1986. The important recommendations of the Council included the following (1) total privatisation of Japan Airlines (2) the introduction of competition in some domestic routes by allowing entry of new carriers (3) to break the monopoly of the JAL in international flights (Yamauchi and Ito, 1996). However, the Council did not recommend the US style deregulation because of the differences in the structure of the airline markets in the US and Japan. Slot restrictions at major airports in Japan were a significant problem and the report recommended that steps should be taken to increase capacity.

The government accepted the policy recommendations of the Council. JAL was fully privatised. ANA was now allowed to serve the international markets. Some domestic city-pair markets were allowed to be served by two or even three carriers. However, entry into a particular city-pair market was allowed only if the number of passengers on that route exceeded a predetermined threshold level.

Further changes were made in 1996. The zone fare system introduced a band within which the carriers are free to set fares. The maximum fare within the zone is calculated on the basis of airline cost and the minimum fare is 25 percent below the maximum fare. However, the carriers are allowed to offer a discount of up to 50 percent of the minimum fare. Even though substantial flexibility is now allowed with respect to airfares, no changes have been made with regard to new entry. New entry is still subject to regulation as before. Capacity at the airports has also remained a problem at some airports. However, the government has taken initiative to increase the capacity at some major airports. Tokyo's Narita airport is being expanded so that it would be able to handle higher traffic. The opening of Kansai international airport increased capacity in the Kansai area (Osaka and surrounding communities like Kyoto and Kobe).

Fares are far from deregulated in Japan even under the new policy. Fares are still set on the basis of distance and do not take any account of the elasticity of demand or peak-load. Even in those routes, which have more than one carrier, the fares are the same for all carriers. Discount fares are increasingly being allowed. However, these discount fares are again the same for all airlines. Entry into the markets still remains a cumbersome process because of the elaborate licensing requirements for the potential carriers. The three airlines have not effectively dealt with restructuring their costs and this makes it difficult for them to cope with domestic deregulation and competition from the airlines in the US. A new airline Skymark started operating in Japan from 1999. This is the first time in 35 years that a new airline started its service. The competition in the Japanese domestic markets has heated up with Skymark Airlines offering heavily discounted fares on many routes and the three major airlines following suit.

Yamauchi (1997) discusses the impact of the regulatory changes on the market structure. The airline companies made huge profits during the boom period of the Japanese economy during the late 1980s. The three big carriers, namely, JAL, ANA and JAS still dominate even though there are nine carriers (including Skymark) serving the domestic and international markets. In addition, there are some commuter and charter carriers. The other five carriers are, however, the subsidiaries of the big three. Air Nippon (ANK) which serves the domestic route and one international route, belongs to ANA. Japan Trans-Ocean Airlines (JTA) and Japan Air Commuter (JAC), offering domestic services, only belong to the JAL and JAS groups respectively. Finally, Japan Asia Airlines (JAA) and NCA, serving international routes only, belong to the JAL and ANA groups respectively.

Before 1986, ANA had the largest share of the domestic market. Since then, JAL has taken over. In some cases, the big three have shifted some of their services to the subsidiaries in order to improve their financial positions. However, there were no dramatic changes in the market share. One reason has been that the capacity at Haneda airport in Tokyo has not seen any changes. However, there has been a marked increase in the number of passengers in those city-pair markets, which are served by two or more carriers. However, as noted before, the services and the fares offered by different airlines have been quite similar and thus, the air travellers have not seen genuine benefits from the changes in the regulatory policies.

27

Some studies find that average cost of airlines has fallen since the 1986 reforms even though the travellers have not benefited from such a fall. The introduction of the zone fare system has not, generally speaking, lowered fares so far.

Although there have been significant changes in the system of regulation in Japan and Japan has moved towards deregulation in recent years, the pace of changes has been too slow compared with what happened in other countries. As Yamauchi (1997) observes, dramatic changes in policies are not characteristic features of the Japanese economy.

Malaysia

Just like many other countries in the region, Malaysia too had a regulated airline market (Oum and Yu, 1998). However, Malaysia has made a number of policy changes.

The origin of the national airline, Malaysian Airlines goes back to 1972 when Malaysia-Singapore Airlines became two separate identities – Malaysian Airlines System and Singapore Airlines. Malaysian Airlines System was renamed Malaysian Airlines in 1987.

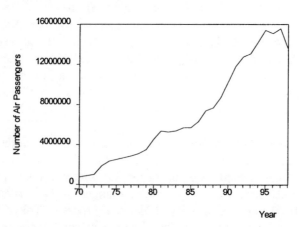

Figure 2.4 Number of Domestic and International Air Passengers in Malaysia, 1970-98
Source: World Bank (2000)

Figure 2.4 shows the number of domestic and international air passengers in Malaysia. In 1970, the number was a modest 0.75 million. The number

28

increased steadily to 15.4 million in 1995, declined to 15.1 million in 1996 and then declined again substantially to 13.7 million in 1998 mainly due to the effects of the Asian crisis.

Malaysian Airlines was partially privatised in 1985 even though the government still continues to hold the 'golden share' which gives it the veto power over major decisions of the airline. Government approval is still needed for any changes in fares. Chairman of Malaysian Airlines Tajudin Ramli's company Naluri Bhd. also holds 29 percent of the shares. Naluri Bhd. is heavily indebted. Foreign ownership limit is now 30 percent and Malaysian Airlines proposed that it be raised to 45 percent. Malaysia's Ministry of Finance has approved the increase in foreign ownership. In practice, 16 percent of the airline owned by the foreigners – Brunei government holds nine percent of the shares. At the end of October 2000, Malaysian Airlines had a debt of $2.63 billion and it was waiting for a restructuring. Its cash-flow problems are mainly the results of loss-making domestic service and the rising fuel costs. The government has not agreed to the airline's proposal to raise domestic fares.

Qantas, KLM and Swissair are reported to be interested in a stake of the Malaysian Airlines at the time of writing. Swissair is emerging to be the main contender. Qantas is out of favour of the government of Malaysia because of the volatile relationship that Malaysia has with Australia. Even with the increase in foreign ownership, the government has no desire to give up its golden share.

Malaysian Airlines signed a memorandum of understanding with the US carrier Northwest for operational and marketing alliance. An open skies agreement with the United States was signed in 1997.

The only other domestic airline in Malaysia is Pelangi Air whose shares are held by the state governments. Pelangi Air serves mostly the tourist destinations.

South Korea

Figure 2.5 shows the number of domestic and international air passengers in South Korea during 1970-1998. It shows the tremendous growth in air passengers for this Asian tiger. The number of air passengers increased at a fast pace from 1.2 million in 1970 to 35.5 million in 1997 but declined to 27 million in 1998 as South Korea was hit hard by the Asian crisis.

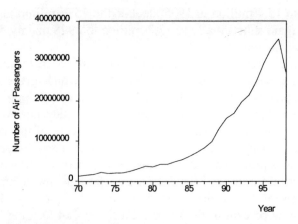

Figure 2.5 Number of Domestic and International Air Passengers in South Korea, 1970-98

Source: World Bank (2000)

South Korea is dominated by three major airlines. These are Korean Airlines, Korean National Airlines and the Asiana Airlines. Korean National Airlines is the government carrier while the other two are private carriers. Asiana was established in 1988. According to Kim (1996), the evolution of regulation of airlines can be divided into two periods: the monopolistic regime (until 1988) and the duopolistic structure (since 1988). The regulation of airlines in South Korea is governed by the Korean Aeronautics Law.

Both entry and exit are still tightly controlled. The entry through the licensing system can be granted if the entry is 'in the public interest', the carrier can meet the safety standards and the entry is justified by market demand. Not only are the entry and exit controlled, airfares were also controlled. Since 1992, however, fares are no longer set by the government. However, any fare changes by the carriers have to be reported to the government. But, such deregulation of airfares has not had much effect because the market for domestic air travel in South Korea has turned into a collusive duopoly.

A number of changes were introduced in 1994. First, the two carriers, Korean Airlines and Korean National Airlines are now free to agree on the allocation of new traffic on different routes. Second, Asiana Airlines is no longer restricted to certain routes. However, entry into a new route still requires approval. Third, if two carriers were to be allowed to serve in a

30

city-pair market, the number of passengers has to be higher than 210,000 for long haul and 180,000 for short haul services respectively. These thresholds are higher than the previous thresholds.

A number of changes also took place in the international air travel arena. South Korea has signed bilateral air service agreements with most of the major countries in the world. The most important of these bilateral agreements have been with the US.

The most important change in the domestic arena has been the entry of Asiana. Since Asiana's entry into the market in 1988, the number of domestic passenger enplanements have increased from 8.7 million to 15.5 million in 1993 (Kim, 1997). However, unlike in the US, the entry did not have any effect on fares.

In short, South Korea has a duopoly in airline markets. The two airlines, KAL and Asiana offer similar kind of service. So, there is not much service competition between the two. Even though the 1996 legislation has allowed fare flexibility, i.e., the airlines can now set fares (they still need to report the fares to the government), price competition has been, so far, negligible at best. This is similar to the situation in Japan. The only difference is that Japan has an oligopoly with three major airlines.

Thailand

Thailand's national airline, Thai Airways International, was created in 1960. Thai Airways International Public Co., Ltd. was set up that year with older aircraft from the Scandinavian Airline Systems (SAS). In exchange, SAS got 30 percent share of the airline (Saggi and Morgan, 1996). In 1977, government of Thailand bought out the shares held by SAS. The national carrier had a merger with the domestic carrier, Thai Airways Co. Ltd. in 1988.

Thai Airways has become a part of the Star alliance involving United and other airlines. Bangkok Airways is only other surviving airline providing domestic services. It serves many tourist destinations. Bangkok Airways, however, is not allowed to compete on routes where Thai Airways serves.

The Angel Airlines, which was the only airline that was allowed to compete with Thai Airways, suspended all its operations in July 2000 for restructuring the company. Angel Airlines started to provide service in September 1999 with three leased aircraft and an initial investment of over one million Baht. Angel faced a number of problems. In recent months, its load factor was around 22 percent – way below the break-even load factor. It faced a number of problems (Anonymous, 2000b). First, it was using aircraft unsuitable for the tourist markets. Second, its employees had morale problems because a large number of employees left to work for other airlines at much better pay and benefits. In June 2000, the salaries of flight attendants were halved. It is possible that Angel Airlines will close its services forever. The government may grant the routes that Angel Airlines served to other airlines. Thai Airways is reported to be negotiating a joint venture with Angel Airlines.

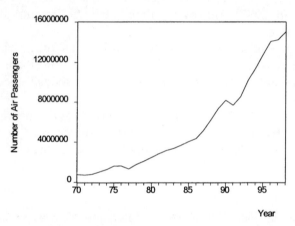

Figure 2.6 Number of Domestic and International Air Passengers in
Thailand, 1970-98
Source: World Bank (2000)

Figure 2.6 shows the number of domestic and international air passengers in Thailand for 1970 to 1998. Being one of the fastest growing Asian countries, Thailand has experienced a tremendous expansion in air traffic. The number of air passengers increased from 0.76 million in 1970 to 8.2 million in 1998. The growth was fastest during the 1990s.

Conclusion

Most Asian countries have experienced a tremendous growth in air passenger transportation during the post war period. The experience of the Asian countries clearly shows that demand for air passenger service is

32

highly income elastic. The 1990s saw a number of important changes in the airline industry in most Asian countries. Almost all the Asian countries have moved towards liberalising air services, although the extent of liberalisation lags behind North America and Oceania.

Chapter 3

Airline Deregulation in Australia and New Zealand

Introduction

In this chapter, we look at the deregulation of airlines in Australia and New Zealand. The main emphasis will be on Australia and not on New Zealand. We take only a cursory look at the experience of New Zealand.

The Australian government gave notice in October 1987 that it would terminate the Airlines Agreement in October 1990 and allow a competitive market to operate. Accordingly, the so-called 'two-airline policy' in interstate aviation in Australia came to an end at midnight on October 30, 1990. Deregulation was introduced through the passage of the Airline Agreement (Termination) Act of 1990. According to the *1990-91 Annual Report* of the Department of Transport and Communications (p. 19), deregulation was:

> ...expected to:
> (a) stimulate growth in the market;
> (b) provide a wide range of airfares and more discounts;
> (c) provide greater incentives for the incumbent and new entrant airlines to become more efficient and more responsive to consumer needs;
> (d) make available a greater variety in the type, standard, and frequency of services.

Evolution of Economic Regulation in Australia

A detailed history of the regulation of airlines in Australia can be found in Brogden (1968), Hocking and Haddon-Cave (1951) and Poulton (1981), among others. A brief sketch of such evolution of airline regulation follows.

The first Act aimed at regulating air transportation in Australia was the Navigation Act of 1920. This Act came into effect on March 28, 1921.

34

Section 4 of the Act gave the Governor-General power to regulate (Poulton, 1981, p. 29):

> (i) for the purpose of carrying out and giving effect to the Paris Convention and the provision of any amendment to the Convention made under Article 34 thereof; and (ii) for the purpose of providing for the control of air navigation in the Commonwealth and Territories.

The Act created confusion regarding the role of the state governments vis-à-vis the Commonwealth government in air transport regulation. The Air Navigation Act of 1920 was amended in 1936 by the Air Navigation Act of 1936. The Commonwealth government was now authorised to control air navigation:
(a) in relation to trade and commerce with other countries and among the states; and
(b) within any territory of the Commonwealth.

The Commonwealth government was thus supposed to keep out of the arena of intra-state aviation. It should be pointed out that territories in Australia are different from the states. These are the Australian Capital Territory (Canberra and surroundings) and the Northern Territory. In practice, however, the Commonwealth government did not keep out of the regulation of intra-state aviation. In fact, there used to be a considerable overlap in Commonwealth and state regulations. The Air Navigation Act of 1947 was passed mainly to approve the ratification of the Chicago Convention in 1944.

The two-airline policy, which ended in 1990, dates back to the 1950s when Robert Menzies was the Prime Minister of Australia. The Menzies government did not want a monopoly to prevail in the provision of the interstate domestic airline service. At the same time, the government thought that it could not support more than two domestic airlines and still maintain efficient operations. Prime Minister Robert Menzies stated this position very clearly in 1949 (quoted in Brogden, 1968, p. 92):

> The government has decided to attempt to secure the retention of the major airlines in competitive service in the Australian community. It is no part of the policy of the government to foster either a government monopoly or a private monopoly on the major air routes. Trans-Australian Airlines has been successfully and efficiently established, and having secured a substantial share of the public goodwill, we consider it desirable that its competition should continue, as long as that competition is fair. Quite frankly, the government

would regard it as unfortunate if either Trans-Australian Airlines or Australian National Airways Propriety Limited.....disappeared from the airline business, since such an event would create either a straight-out government monopoly or a private monopoly, to which each this government and, we believe, the public, are in principle opposed.

While the above quotation is from a typical political speech, it does summarise the philosophy of the Menzies government. Although the Prime Minster was the main contributor to this policy, the credit for this policy is variously attributed to the Prime Minister, to the Director-General of Civil Aviation (Air Marshall Sir Richard Williams) and to the Department of Civil Aviation and Air generally. In 1952, to legislatively enshrine the official two-airline policy, the Civil Aviation Agreement Act was passed. Under this policy, two carriers, Trans-Australia Airlines (TAA), a government firm and Australian National Airways (ANA) operated side by side. To provide a fair deal, the Act gave concessions to ANA. The government undertook to guarantee all loans raised by ANA up to a certain limit. During the early years of TAA, public servants could travel only by that company. However, ANA was deemed to be the weaker airline and later given part of the government's business. ANA faced financial difficulties and was taken over by Ansett Transport Industries (ATI) in 1957. The passing of the Civil Aviation Agreement Act 1957 further strengthened the two-airline policy by declaring that one of the objectives of the Commonwealth government was to secure and maintain a position in which there were two, and not more than two, operators of trunk airline services. The Act set up a Rationalisation Committee to exert control over the industry. The Committee consisted of a member from each of the two airlines plus a co-ordinator nominated by the Transport Minister. In 1958, the Airlines Equipment Act was passed. This Act was designed to control the size and composition of the fleets; it authorised the government to restrict the fleets of each operator to cater for 50 percent of the traffic on competitive routes.

In 1961, two major pieces of legislation were passed. The Airlines Agreement Act aimed at creating an atmosphere in which "planned competition on the major routes could continue with consequent benefit to the operators, to the travelling public and to the nation". The Act set out more precisely the matters to be controlled by the Rationalisation Committee: timetables, frequencies and stopping places; aircraft types and capacity, proposed variations in fare and freight levels; and load factors in relation to particular groups of routes. The Act provided that no jet plane would be ordered prior to 8 November 1962 and none would be placed into service before 1 January 1964. The two carriers agreed to introduce their first and second jet aircraft concurrently with the other's first and second jets (Davies, 1971). The Australian National Airline Act of 1961 introduced new controls for TAA following protests from Ansett that TAA did not need to pay any dividend. The Act provided that a target rate of dividend was to be set each year.

A turning point in the history of airline regulation in Australia was marked in 1981. There were severe criticisms of the policies from many quarters. Fare structures were seen as unjust. There were special concerns about the issue of short-haul routes being subsidised by long-haul routes. The Holcroft Inquiry (1981) examined the issue of cross-subsidy in detail. The Inquiry (Holcroft, 1981, vol 1, p. 14) also observed:

> In the circumstances, it has been difficult in framing practical recommendations on air-fare pricing to have much regard to the government's stated 'objective of increasing competition'. Almost anywhere the Inquiry has attempted to do this, it has run virtually impenetrable barrier of the provisions of the Two Airlines Agreement, existing or proposed.

Although the Holcroft Inquiry favoured market solutions, it saw itself constrained by the two-airline policy. Among the policy recommendations accepted by the government, the following were important:

(a) implementation of a pricing formula based on cost. This formula would comprise of the flag-fall and the distance rate of the national network;

(b) implementation of a pricing policy which would be nationally consistent;

(c) discount fares to be left to be determined by the airlines and only an economy core fare to be determined.

Also, a wide range of discount fares would be made available.

Trans-Australia Airlines (later called Australian Airlines) was made a public company in 1981. However, the Commonwealth government still retained effective ownership. Three more important Acts were passed in 1981. The Independent Air Fares Committee Act set up the Independent Air Fares Committee, which was made responsible for setting air fares. The fares were to be related to cost as far as possible and cross-subsidies were to be avoided. In determining fares, the effect of such fares on quantity demanded was to be taken into account. Major air-fare reviews (for a fare increase of more than 5 percent since the last review) could be initiated by a carrier at any time. But if the Committee were to initiate such reviews, six months had to elapse between the two reviews. The Committee was also to approve discount fares. It was required that discount fares should increase profitability of a carrier and that such discount fares would not increase the economy fares. The discount fares were to be implemented in a non-discriminatory manner among persons or classes of persons. The Committee attempted to incorporate efficiency considerations into air-fare determination. It used two types of core fare formulas (May, 1986).

The Airline Equipment Amendment Act of 1981 amended the Airlines Equipment Act of 1958. It strengthened the control of entry into the industry through a better licensing scheme of aircraft imports. While the previous Act applied only to Australian Airlines and Ansett Australia, the new Act sought to control the capacity of regional and cargo operators. Under the Act, the regional and commuter airlines and were allowed to import large turbojet aircraft provided that these aircraft were not re-deployed in such uses which would undermine the two-airline policy. East-West Airlines (a major commuter carrier) imported medium-sized jet aircraft as a result of this Act.

An Assessment of the Performance under the Two-Airline Policy

The two-airline policy in Australia had been the subject of scrutiny for a very long time. The list of contributions have been varied and many. Important earlier studies include the Bureau of Transport Economics (1985), Davies (1971 and 1977), Department of Transport (1979), Forsyth (1979 and 1991), Forsyth and Hocking (1980), Holcroft (1981), Kirby (1979, 1981 and 1982), May (1986) and Wettenhall (1962).

In any assessment of the performance under the two-airline policy, it is almost natural to compare the situation to the pre-deregulation days in the United States. But, as Forsyth (1991) points out, there were some important differences in the two-regulatory frameworks. In the United States, although entry into routes and into the industry was controlled, there was hardly any attempt to control capacity. Since price competition was restricted, one form of service competition was schedule competition – the result was a low load factor on many routes. In Australia, however, capacity was regulated resulting in high load factors. Load factors were kept high in Australia because poorly booked flights were cancelled.

Implicit in the government policy was the belief that there were substantial economies of scale in the operation of the air service. However, empirical evidence did not seem to support this view. The Treasury, for example, argued that once the minimum efficient scale of operations was achieved, there were hardly any further economies of scale (May, 1986).

Economies of vehicle scale is a different matter altogether. Evidence strongly suggests that the larger the aircraft, other things like load factors being equal, the lower is the unit cost especially for the long haul (Graham and Kaplan, 1982). Also, empirical evidence suggest that the existence of economies of density whereby unit cost is reduced when airlines add flights or add seats to existing flights if load factors remain the same (Caves, Christensen and Tretheway, 1984).

The 'no-entry' policy of the government was implemented by its refusal to grant import licenses to potential competitors. Only Ansett Australia and Australian Airlines were granted such licenses. In the absence of large aircraft manufacturers in Australia, potential competitors were basically barred from entering the markets. Besides entry control, the capacity was tightly controlled as well to prevent what the Commonwealth government deemed as 'wasteful competition'.

The Australian two-airline policy was dubbed a success by many who argued that it was a stable situation and the safety record was quite good. The airlines did enjoy financial stability and consistent profits. However, Australians who travelled to the United States after the passage of the U.S. Airline Deregulation Act of 1978 complained bitterly about the higher air fares at home. Although the Australian two-airline policy was a apparently a duopoly, in practice, it acted like a monopoly where the two carriers had a tacit collusion. However, there were attributes of competition as well. For example, Hocking and Forsyth (1982) argue that parallel scheduling whereby the two airlines had flights to same destinations that were taking off almost at the same time was a sign of competition rather than of a monopoly.

The level of airfares under regulation had been a matter of much concern. In fact, much of the pressure for reform came from the perception of the travelling public that airfares in Australia had been high, especially when compared to similar routes in the United States. Comparisons of Australian and U.S. airfares had been fashionable but such comparisons had many limitations. The Bureau of Transport Economics (1985) identified a number of limitations. The first and most obvious limitation was that exchange rates had been fluctuating a great deal, making it difficult to compare such airfares. Second, the U.S. airfare structure was quite complex. Standard coach fares on routes of similar distance were used as a basis for comparison; but such comparisons were misleading because the percentage of travellers on coach fares was much lower than in the United States than in Australia. Third, distance was not the only variable determining the airfares in the United States after deregulation. Any sample would, therefore, be biased because in a competitive environment, the price/quality combination would be expected to vary on routes of similar distance. Finally, interpreting the data could be difficult. The differences in airfares in the two countries might be due partly to the demand and supply conditions in the two countries. Supply-side factors may include differences in safety regulations, the cost of such inputs as labour and other institutional arrangements.

There are two basic approaches to comparing the airfares in Australia with those in the United States. One is average yield (cents per revenue passenger-kilometre) and the other is the comparison of fares on selected routes. Average yield avoids the bias involved in the selection of fare types or routes. If the yields of those US airlines that were similar in size to the two domestic interstate carriers in Australia are compared, they show that operating yields were much higher for the two Australian airlines. In a comparison on routes of similar distances, Trengrove (1985) finds that in 1982, Australian airfares were, on average, 21 percent higher than U.S. fares.

Table 3.1 compares some of the performance indicators of comparable U.S. airlines and Australian Airlines and Ansett for 1983-84.

Table 3.1 Performance Indicators of Selected Airlines in Australia and the US

Airline	Expenses per available tonne-km (Australian cents)	Expenses per revenue passenger-km (Australian cents)	Passenger-km per employee (thousand km)
Australian	89.8	13.6	545
Ansett	74.6	11.8	582
Air California	53.6	11.8	1,251
Frontier	50.1	10.2	1,233
Ozark	49.7	11.6	1,066
People Express	36.1	5.1	3,040
Southwest	30.1	6.8	2,074

Source: Bureau of Transport Economics (1985), pp. 70-71

Table 3.1 shows that operating expenses per available tonne-kilometre and operating expenses per revenue passenger-kilometres were higher for Australian and Ansett than for U.S. airlines of a comparable size for the year 1983-84. On the other hand, passenger-kilometres per employee were lower for Australian and Ansett. This supports an earlier study by Kirby (1979) who found that the two airlines in Australia were characterised by higher costs and lower labour productivity.

Airline Deregulation

It must be pointed out that although there had been only two interstate airlines, there were about forty-five regional and commuter airlines. However, with the advent of interstate airline deregulation in 1990, the distinctions between different types of airlines became somewhat blurred. Increasingly, these carriers were now being allowed to carry interstate passengers - in some cases, to destinations where the two interstate carriers did not fly. In most cases, however, these airlines had the same owners as the two interstate airlines. Green (1990, p. 25) notes:

41

In casting the net for the smaller operators, the Big Two have followed an example set by airlines in the United States, where strong feeder networks are important.

In fact, out of 45 commuter airlines, 20 were associated with Ansett, either by equity or by commercial arrangements. Out of the remaining 25, 15 had links with Australian Airlines. According to the Department of Transport and Communications (1990-91), the top ten commuter airlines, accounting for up to 90 percent of total commuter traffic, were linked either with Ansett or with Australian Airlines (now Qantas).

The immediate pre-deregulation years were marked by mergers and take-overs by both Australian and Ansett. For example, East-West Airline was taken over by TNT/News Corporation (owner of Ansett Australia) in July 1987. Ansett also established Ansett Express in 1991. Australian acquired Eastern Australian, Sunstate Mildura and Sunstate Queensland airlines in 1990. It also launched Australian Airlink in 1991. Many of the take-overs had been in Queensland. Queensland is a premier destination of interstate and overseas tourists in Australia. Therefore, a share of the air passenger market in Queensland is of strategic importance to an expanding airline.

In the next part the effects of airline deregulation are analysed under four different headings: (a) the economic effects of deregulation on air passenger traffic, fares and flight frequencies; (b) the contestability of markets; (c) entries and exits under deregulation; (d) intermodal competition and (e) overall impact. Sinha and Sinha (1993) has a brief discussion of the various aspects of the impacts of airline deregulation.

Passenger Traffic, Fares and Flight Frequencies

The number of passengers carried domestically surpassed all previous records during the first few years after deregulation. The overall growth of origin-destination (O-D) passengers from September 1990 to December 1991 was 66 percent according to the Price Surveillance Authority (1992-93). The number of O-D passengers on the main interstate routes increased from about 1,800,000 to about 2,800,000 during the same period. Compass Airlines, which entered the interstate market on 1 December 1990, steadily increased its number of passengers it carried until it ceased operation (of its first entry into the market) on 16 December 1991. Polls showed that there was an increase in the percentage of first-time travellers during the first year of deregulation. From December 1991 to June 1992, the number of O-D passengers fell by about 13 percent (although it was higher during the period immediately before deregulation). The fall can be attributed partly to the exit of Compass Airline, which was offering discount fares much below those being offered by Australian and Ansett. The exit of Compass caused a marked decrease in the industry capacity. Consequently, there was a substantial increase in the load factor. The load factor increased from 69.4 percent during the January-March 1991 quarter to 79.8 percent during the January-March 1992 quarter. Between June 1992 and December 1992, the number of O-D passengers increased by about 14 percent (Compass re-entered the market in August 1992).

Table 3.2 shows the changes in average and economy fares during September 1990 and December 1991.

Table 3.2 Movements in Average and Economy Fares: September 1990 to December 1991 (in percent)

City pair	Average Fare	Economy Fare
Adelaide/Melbourne	-26.9	+15.1
Adelaide/Perth	-35.4	+12.2
Brisbane/Melbourne	-29.8	+13.1
Canberra/Sydney	-26.2	+14.7
Brisbane/Sydney	+0.5	+19.5
Coolangatta/Sydney	-22.3	+21.6
Hobart/Melbourne	-14.8	+14.9
Melbourne/Perth	-41.3	+11.9
Melbourne/Sydney	-30.1	+14.7
Perth/Sydney	-41.3	+11.6

Source: Price Surveillance Authority (1992-93)

The average airfares fell in almost all city-pair markets between September 1990 and December 1991. Canberra/Sydney was an exception. The highest fall was in the Melbourne/Perth and Sydney/Perth markets where the average fares fell by 41.3 percent in both cases. At the same time, the economy fare rose by more than ten percent in all cases. This clearly shows that economy fares were becoming less relevant after deregulation. Indeed, the Price Surveillance Authority found that during the twelve-month period of 1991, the number of passengers paying full economy fares had more than halved; in fact, less than 25 percent of the passengers paid full economy fares. It should be pointed out, however, that not all of the fare reductions could be attributed to increased competition. Some of the fare reductions could be attributed to the downturn of the economy (Bureau of Transport Economics, 1991a). It must also be pointed out that the decrease in average fares was not limited to those routes where Compass was serving, although the magnitude of the fall was higher on those routes.

Since December 1991, the movements in fares have been uneven. For example, during the September-December 1992 quarter, average fare increased on 15 routes (among the top 21 interstate routes) in the range of 0.1 to 11.5 percent, while the average fare fell from 1.2 and 3 percent on six routes. This general increase in the average fares meant that the new discount fares offered by the airlines were offset by increased economy fares and changes in the composition of travellers. Although the average fares increased on many routes during the last quarter of 1992, these were below pre-deregulation average fares in nominal terms.

On 6 November, the Price Surveillance Authority (which used to monitor airfares) and the Trade Prices Commission was merged to form the Australian Competition and Consumer Commission (ACCC). ACCC still monitors airfares. Of course, there is no regulation of airfares on its part. In a 1996 report, the ACCC finds that since the departure of Compass from the market, there had been a reduction in price competition. Qantas and Ansett were found to have almost identical airfares. The average airfares and discount airfares had been gradually increasing. Thus, the competition between the two airlines had been mostly with regard to service. By examining the operations of the airlines between September 1990 and September 1995, the report finds the following.

First, there was a drop of 8.7 percent in real and 10.8 percent in nominal terms in the average airfares during the five-year period. During the period when Compass was in operation, the fall in the airfares were the most significant. In nominal terms, the average airfares fell by 31.6 percent when Compass was in operation the first time; during the period of its second run, the average airfares fell by 21 percent. However, while the average airfares fell by 11.1 percent on the long distance routes, the average airfares on the short distance routes increased by 3.1 percent. The full economy fares increased between 15 and 35 percent during the same period. However, the percentage of people paying the full economy fare fell from 50 percent to 20 percent.

Second, as expected, a decline in the average airfares led to an increase in the number of air passengers. The growth was phenomenal. It increased from 8.9 to 14 million during the period, an increase of 57 percent. Again, the growth was highest when Compass was operating.

Third, the deregulatory period was also marked by improved yield management system, better terminal facilities and the introduction of frequent flier programs.

Figure 3.1 Business, Economy and Discount Airfare Indexes from the Fourth Quarter of 1992 to the Second Quarter of 2000

Source:　　Bureau of Transport Economics (2000)

Figure 3.1 shows the indexes of business, economy and discount airfares from the fourth quarter of 1992 to the second quarter of 2000. All indexes have a base of 4th quarter 1992. The discount fare index reached the lowest level in the 2nd quarter of 1996 when it was 85. The discount fare index showed much more fluctuations than the other two indexes. The business fare index showed almost a steady increase while the economy fare index was almost steady.

Airline deregulation in the United States resulted in an increase in flight frequency in many city-pair markets. An increase in flight frequency has a two-fold effect on service quality: it increases the travellers' choice of departure times; it also increases the probability of being able to book a flight at a short notice.

Flight frequencies increased not only on those routes in which Compass was serving but on other routes as well. During the first year of deregulation, flight frequency increased by 16 percent on the top forty routes. If Compass is excluded, the increase in flight frequency was 11 percent during the same period (see Bureau of Transport and Communications Economics, 1991b). Of course, the exit of Compass adversely affected the flight frequencies on those routes in which Compass was serving.

Contestability of Markets

There is no doubt that the favourable effects of airline deregulation in the United States gave a positive impetus for deregulation in Australia. For a discussion of the applicability of the contestability theory to the deregulated US airline markets, see chapter 7 and Sinha (1986). Theoretically, the contestable market theory as proposed by Baumol, Panzar and Willig (1982) justified airline deregulation. In Australia, rigorous testing of the contestability theory is difficult for several important reasons. First, Australia's population is less than ten percent of that of the United States. Consequently, the number of major airline markets is small compared with the U.S. markets. Second, deregulation did not produce an influx of new airlines into the interstate markets. The only airline that entered following deregulation and later exited the deregulated markets was Compass Airline. However, in 2000, Virgin Blue and Impulse entered the interstate markets. Third, fares and other data are not readily available.

However, two important studies have been conducted to test the level of competitiveness in airline markets in Australia. The first study by Starkie and Starrs (1984) was undertaken before interstate airline deregulation. The study deals with intra-state airline markets in South Australia. Victoria and South Australia are two states where there are no state controls over intra-state aviation. But, before 1979, the Commonwealth government controlled intra-state airline markets using Air

Navigation Act of 1920. At the recommendation of the Domestic Air Transport Policy Reviews, the Commonwealth government virtually removed these controls in 1979. As a result, the intra-state airline markets in South Australia and Victoria became much more competitive. The authors use cross-section data for sixty-two city-pair markets in South Australia for May 1983. To test the contestability hypothesis, the authors regress the basic one-way economy fare against great circle distance and a dummy variable which took the value of one, if the route had more than one operator, and the value of zero otherwise. They find the dummy variable to be statistically insignificant, meaning that there was no significant difference in the fares between monopoly routes and non-monopoly routes. The results, therefore, seemed to suggest the validity of the contestability theory. However, they find little evidence of the hit-and-run entry. About half of the routes included in the regression were monopolies, and these seemed sustainable. Their findings, however, do not apply to the interstate airline markets because of the differences in the type and scale of operations.

The second study was undertaken more recently and used data for interstate service (Bureau of Transport Economics, 1991b). At the interstate level, whatever causal evidence is available seems to suggest that actual competition matters more than potential competition. The average airfares went down more in those routes where Compass was competing than in those routes where it was not. The study fits the following equation for testing the effects of airline deregulation on competition:

$$\log(FARE) = \log(K) + A.\log(DIST) + B.\log(COMP) + C.\log(YDUM) + D.\log(PAX) \tag{7.1}$$

where FARE is maximum discount fare or in some cases, maximum discount fares per kilometres, DIST is the great circle distance, COMP is the number of competitors on the route, YDUM is the Compass dummy variable, PAX is the number of 'uplift-discharge passengers' and K is the constant term. The equation was fitted to cross-section data for the top one hundred city pairs of the year ending December 1991. The fares were from the best available discount fares during the June/July/August fare war. The results are in table 3.3.

Table 3.3 Regression Results for Discount Fares

Dependent variable	K	DIST	COMP	YDUM	PAX	R^2
Discount fare	0.99 (0.26)	0.53 (13.0)	-0.21 (-3.80)	-0.25 (-2.61)	-0.04 (-1.78)	0.73
Discount fare	1.58 (0.26)	0.54 (14.9)	-0.26 (-5.10)	-0.31 (-3.45)	----	0.72
Discount fare per kilometre	1.99 (0.26)	-0.47 (-13.1)	-0.21 (-3.80)	-0.25 (-2.61)	-0.04 (-1.78)	0.75
Discount fare per kilometre	1.58 (0.26)	-0.47 (-12.8)	-0.26 (-5.10)	-0.26 (-3.45)	----	0.74

Note: Bracketed figures are t-statistics except for the constant terms for which they are standard errors

Source: Bureau of Transport and Communications Economics (1991b)

COMP and YDUM are both negative and significant. Thus, the competition between Australian and Ansett had the effect of reducing discount fares. Additionally, the presence of Compass on a route had the effect of reducing the discount fares. One important limitation of the study is that it used fare data for the period of a very intensive price war. A study can, of course, be sensitive to the fare data that are chosen.

Entries and Exits under Deregulation

The deregulation of interstate airlines in Australia resulted in one airline entering the market almost immediately following deregulation. Compass Airline began operations on 1 December 1990 and ceased operations on 16 December 1991. Southern Cross bought the Compass logo in 1992 and began operating as Compass Airline on 31 August 1992. It had an even shorter life span. It went out of business on 12 March 12 1993. The details about the entries and exits of Compass can be found in Sinha and Sinha (1994a).

Since Compass had a very crucial role to play during the first few years of deregulation, it is worthwhile to ask what could be the reasons for its failure. Compass enjoyed an enormous amount of public support and it is unfortunate that it failed, especially when all indications seem to point out that actual competition matters more than potential competition.

Compass, in both of its incarnations, failed due to several reasons. According to Douglas and Cunningham (1992), Compass, during its first run, made strategic mistakes in its choice of aircraft (using larger aircraft), in overestimating demand, in underestimating its rivals, in providing only one-class service (it did introduce business class service in its second run) and in its yield management.

Two more airlines have entered the domestic airline market in Australia. These are Impulse Airlines and Virgin Blue (owned by Richard Branson). Impulse was the first to enter. Virgin Blue had its first flights on 31 August 2000 flying Sydney-Brisbane and Brisbane-Melbourne routes. The entry of these two airlines has been marked by fare wars during the late 2000.

Intermodal Competition

The U.S. experience shows that intermodal competition increased substantially after the passing of the Airline Deregulation Act in 1978. The two major bus companies, Greyhound and Trailways, had to cut prices in order to attract customers who were lured away by the cheap fares. Amtrak (the rail company) introduced special deals for passengers. In Australia, the level of competition between air travel and land travel (bus, train and car) was very low until airline deregulation. Data on intermodal competition are not available in any great detail. The study by the Bureau of Transport and Communications Economics (1991b) finds that intermodal competition had increased. In response to cheap flights offered by the airlines, the major bus companies lowered prices. A comparison of the discount fares offered by the major airlines with the fares offered by bus/rail companies is fraught with difficulties. First, there are many restrictions on airfares; for example, booking and payment for many tickets need to be made at least three weeks in advance; Bus/rail tickets are less restrictive. Second, some of the discount air tickets may be sold out very quickly and consequently not available for latecomers.

Overall Impact

As expected, airline deregulation in Australia has had the effect of increasing price competition. It also increased intermodal competition. The number of people taking air trips increased substantially since deregulation. It is obvious that the full effects of deregulation will be realised over the long run. Unlike in the United States, hub and spoke operations, which lead to better capacity utilisation and reduced costs, did not develop in Australia after deregulation. Two major explanations for this are: the smaller population in Australia means a lower volume of traffic; over 90 percent of the population live in five major metropolitan areas making the rest of the country 'too thin' in population for sustainable air traffic.

Other Changes

A number of changes have taken place in recent years. In March 1993, British Airways bought 25 percent of the shares of Qantas. A public float for the remainder of the shares took place in July 1995 thus fully privatising Qantas. In 1994, Australian Airlines became a wholly owned subsidiary of Qantas – the national carrier of Australia. Ansett started offering international services in September 1993. It is now called Ansett International. 49 percent of the ownership of Ansett International is with Ansett Holdings which is owned entirely by Air New Zealand.

Australia has moved aggressively on privatising the airports. The airports in Brisbane, Melbourne and Perth have already been privatised and other airports are under consideration for privatisation. All the other major airports are now owned by the Federal Airports Corporation and are in the process of being privatised.

In contrast, the majority of the airports in the United States continue to be owned by the local governments and the federal government remains the most important source of revenue for the airports. There does not seem to be any urgency in privatising the airports long after airline deregulation had taken place.

Airline Deregulation in New Zealand

Airline deregulation in New Zealand preceded the deregulation in Australia. A 1983 legislation abolished the government control of fares and entry barriers (Findlay and Kissling, 1998). The broader scheme of reducing the size of the New Zealand government was adopted in 1984. Since then, a number of steps were taken to deregulate the airline industry. The national carrier, Air New Zealand was privatised in 1989. To spur competition in the domestic markets, Australia-based Ansett was invited by the government to set up a subsidiary called Ansett New Zealand (Jaggi and Morgan, 1996). In addition, another airline, Kiwi Airline started services between Australian and New Zealand cities in 1995. Kiwi was competing aggressively with Air New Zealand. However, Kiwi's operations came to a halt in March 1996.

Since Australia and especially New Zealand have low population, it makes sense if the Australia and New Zealand combine their market to promote more competition and offer better services to the air travellers. The bilateral co-operation in air service between Australia and New Zealand started in 1961 when an agreement was signed. However, the agreement and the subsequent memoranda of understanding were highly restrictive in nature (Findlay and Kissling, 1998). Fares, frequencies and capacity were determined by the Australian and New Zealand governments. There were only two airlines, Qantas and Air New Zealand, which were allowed to fly between the two countries. However, a memorandum of understanding signed in 1992 made significant changes. These included (a) a possible creation of a joint block being established for negotiating international traffic rights (b) freedom of airlines to fix their frequencies and fares (c) for both cargo and passengers, multiple designation to be allowed.

At present, 44 percent of Air New Zealand's operating costs are in US dollars. The slump in the value of New Zealand dollar which shows no sign of any recovery creates problems for New Zealand. Air New Zealand expects that additional benefits will be realised in the near future from its Ansett Holdings. Air New Zealand joined the Star alliance some time ago. Singapore Airlines now holds a 25 percent stake in the airline.

Qantas is now involved in providing domestic service in New Zealand through the newly emerged Qantas New Zealand. This is a franchise agreement which followed after a potential deal for buying into the Ansett New Zealand fell through (Thomas, 2000).

Conclusions

As pointed out by Findlay (1996), at least two issues with regard to the Trans-Tasman single aviation market are yet to be resolved. First, there are the issues involving immigration and safety. Second, the issue of beyond right has not yet been dealt with.

Chapter 4

Airline Regulation and Deregulation in Canada

Introduction

Being a relatively small country and adjacent to the United States, the distinction between domestic airlines and international airlines in Canada is somewhat blurred. Two major carriers dwarf the activities of the other airlines. These are Air Canada and Canadian Airlines International.

Air transportation plays a crucial role in the Canadian economy because even though Canada has a vast landmass, its population is only 26 million. A comparison of the passenger-kilometres, GDP and population can show the relative increase in air travel. Figure 4.1 shows three indices – those of air passengers-kilometres, GDP (in real terms) and population with a base of 1961=1 for the period from 1961 to 1998. During this 38-year period, GDP and population have increased 3.61-fold and 1.66-fold respectively. However, during the same period, air passenger-kilometres have increased 17.75-fold.

Figure 4.2 shows the index numbers of employees in Canada for air transportation, for the whole economy and for transportation in general. The index numbers have a base of 1961=1. The number of employees involved in air transportation increased from 17,700 in 1961 to 52,896 in 1997. While the number of employees in the air transportation increased three-fold, the number of employees for the whole economy and for transportation increased by 114 percent and 33 percent respectively. The total number of employees in the transportation sector includes the number of employees in air transportation. During the period from 1961 to 1997, the share of employees in the air transportation as a percentage of total employees in the transportation sector has increased from 5.2 percent in 1961 to 11.7 percent in 1997. As a percentage of total employment in Canada, the share of the employees in air transportation increased from 0.34 percent to 0.47 percent.

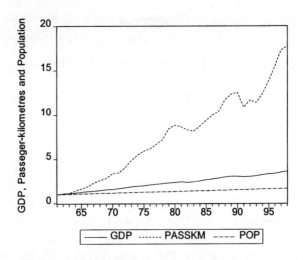

Figure 4.1 Growth of Real GDP, Air Passenger Kilometres and Population, 1961-98

Source: Transport Canada website (2000)

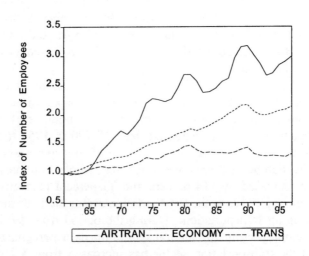

Figure 4.2 Index Numbers of Employees in the Economy, Transportation and Air Transportation, 1961-98

Source: Transport Canada website (2000)

Airline Regulation and Deregulation in Canada

The Canadian system of regulation of airlines somewhat paralleled the US until the later part of 1970s when the US completely deregulated its airlines. Thus, while in the United States, deregulation took place in a relatively short period of time, Canada, in contrast, adopted a gradual approach towards deregulation.

Evolution of Regulation

The regulation of the Canadian airlines began in 1919 when the Federal Air Board was established to certify pilots and aircraft (Goldberg, 1994). However, the introduction of an airline had to wait until 1926 when the Western Canada Airways (WCA) was established by James Richardson who is called the 'Father of Canadian Aviation'. WCA was growing rapidly by extending its services beyond northern Ontario west to the islands of the pacific coast and north to the arctic ocean. WCA was fast becoming the world's leading air freight company transporting furs and fish south and miners and supplies north. As WCA was reigning supreme in western Canada, a number of aviation companies in eastern Canada beset by financial woes were attracting a number of American companies who were interested in buying these companies at cheap prices and getting a foothold into the Canadian market. Richardson helped form the Aviation Corporation of Canada by consolidating four of the financially troubled companies. The three shareholders in the company were the Canadian Pacific (CP), the government owned Canadian National Railways (CNR) and Richardson. Next came the merger of the Aviation Corporation of Canada and the WCA in 1930 and the new company was named Canadian Airways. Later in 1942, CP consolidated its position by buying out others' shares in the Canadian Airways and renaming it as the Canadian Pacific Airways (CPA).

Meanwhile, the idea of a national airline was taking shape. Canadians had always been living under the threat of being swamped by the Americans and airline business was no exception. A national airline would help thwart the airlines in the US to dominate the Canadian markets. More than 80 percent of Canada's population live within 200 miles of the border with the US. With the election of the Liberals in 1935, the time was ripe for the establishment of a national airline. At first, the plan was to have the airline as a public/private ownership with Richardson's company holding the private shares but at the insistence of Transport Minister Clarence

55

Howe, it was established as a wholly-owned subsidiary of CNR in 1937 and it was called the Trans-Canada Airlines (TCA). Ironically, the first route to be served by TCA was between Vancouver and Seattle. CPA was arguing for a merger with TCA, which never materialised. In 1943, the King declared that only TCA was authorised to offer international air services.

Economic regulation, in the true sense of the term, started in 1938 when the Transport Act of 1938 was passed. Earlier, the Department of Transport had been established in 1936. By this Act, the existing Board of Railway Commissioners was renamed the Board of Transport Commissioners. The Commission's authority was to cover airline route operations, rates and schedules. The 1938 Act gave the Board the authority to grant a license for new air service if the service were to be found necessary for 'public convenience and necessity' (Baldwin, 1975). The Board was to give preferences to those services, which were complimentary rather than competitive in nature. The rationale behind such regulation was to prevent destructive competition. It was believed that regulation would lead to lower rather than higher airfares because it would eliminate destructive competition. As noted earlier, the consolidation within the airline industry meant that besides TCA, only CPA (sometimes called CP) became virtually the only other surviving major carrier. The role of the Board as a regulatory agency fundamentally changed with the duopoly in the airline services. CPA's parent company, the Canadian Pacific Railways started to exert considerable pressure on the government (Baldwin, 1975).

In 1944, a specific agency for dealing with airlines was created – Air Transport Board. The Board was given substantial powers to regulate the industry. With the exception of TCA for which licenses would be automatic, all air service providers would have to receive licenses to operate. The Board had the right to prescribe rates, schedules, the types of aircraft and the routes to be followed. Unlike the regulatory regime in the US, which aimed at fostering competition in the airline service, regulation in Canada never had such a goal. However, the goal of trying to protect the interests of the existing carriers was common to the regulatory philosophy in both countries.

The Liberals' rule ended in 1957 when the Conservative Party came back to power for the first time after 1935. The Conservative Party had been advocating for more competition in the provision of airline services all along. At the insistence of the new Prime Minister, charter operations and speciality licenses for aircraft weighing less than 2,500 pounds were decontrolled in 1958; in 1959, the same classes of service providers weighing up to 18,000 pounds were decontrolled. The effect was swift – there was an immediate increase in the number of carriers providing those types of services. The Air Transport Industries Association reacted by insisting that the old regulations be re-imposed. The Board was favouring the regulations as well on two counts: such controls would help it to regain the powers it had and such regulations would cross-subsidise one group of customers.

TCA was re-named Air Canada in 1964. Air Canada was granted monopoly on all domestic transcontinental routes by the government for the period between 1937 and 1959. The routes and fares recommended by Air Canada were approved by the government until 1978. In 1978, the special treatment meted out to Air Canada was stopped. An act passed in 1978 required that all airlines including Air Canada would be subject to same regulations.

The National Transportation Act was passed in 1967. By this Act, the Canadian Transport Commission (CTC) was created and Air Transport Board was merged with the CTC. However, there were no major changes in the system of airline regulation.

The Air Canada Act was passed in February 1977. The ownership of Air Canada was transferred from the Canadian National Railways to the federal government by this Act.

Effects of Airline Regulation

Jordan (1979) observes that during the period from 1938 to 1978, national carriers in USA and Canada were subject to the same full regulation with regard to entry, exit and prices. However, there were some differences in the regulation in the two countries. First, in addition to regulation with respect to entry, exit and prices, Canadian airlines were subject to service quality regulation whereas regulation with regard to service was not permitted under CAB regulation. Second, in Canada, airline regulation covered a far more extended range of operators. All commercial operators – operating inter-provincial and intra-provincial services were subject to regulation. In the US, intrastate, contract and speciality carriers and flying clubs and schools were not subject to regulation. In fact, in another study, Jordan (1970) has shown that the intrastate flights (which were not subject to regulation) had lower fares than the interstate flights of the same length in the US, which raise doubts as to whether regulation was protecting the air travellers. Third, until the early 1970s, airlines in the US could not upgrade their services. In contrast, in Canada, the Canadian Pacific became a major carrier operating major transcontinental and international routes from its humble beginning serving north-south regional routes. In addition, there was another difference in the regulation in Canada and the United States. Jordan feels that the CAB had much more independence than its Canadian counterpart.

Jordan's conclusion about the effect of such regulation on fares is obvious. Fares would have been lower without regulation. Obviously, Canadian airline regulation had its effects on entries and exits, as did the regulation of the CAB in the United States. In both cases, regulation resulted in a lower number of carriers and promoted mergers as a means of exit.

Airline Deregulation

Canada moved towards liberalising its airlines. It will be instructive to compare the case of Canadian liberalisation with that of the US airline deregulation. The first attempt at liberalising the regulation of airlines in Canada was taken in May 1984 when the Minister of Transport announced the 'New Canadian Air Transport Policy' (Minister of Transport, 1984). Canada was now divided into two regions: north and south. The policy aimed at deregulating the air service in the densely populated south but not in the sparsely populated north. Restrictions on capacity, frequency of service and equipment types were removed (Pustay, 1999). Carriers were now free to reduce fares without needing any approval but they could increase fares only to the extent of the increase in the consumer price index. However, these changes did not result in an influx of entry. Most city-pair markets were still being served by one or two airlines. The result was that there was no decrease in the overall concentration in the domestic market. The National Transportation Act, which came into effect on 1 January 1988, introduced almost total deregulation in the south – this is the region bordering the US where the overwhelming majority of the Canadians live. In the north, however, the carriers would still be subject to controls over entry, fares and other conditions of service as before (Oum and Yu, 1998). The government removed most of the regulatory restrictions on the existing airlines. However, this liberalisation did not lead to no control over entry.

Entry into the Canadian markets remained under the control of Air Transport Committee of the Canadian Transport Commission which was in charge of rates and fares as well. Domestic carriers are still protected from competition from foreign carriers serving Canadian routes and US-Canada transborder routes.

Compared with the vast number of studies on the effects of airline deregulation in the US, there have been only a handful number of studies on the effects of airline deregulation in Canada. Compared with the vast US markets, Canadian city-pair markets are smaller and a lot fewer in number. That explains the paucity of studies only partially. The other reason is that data on airlines in Canada have not been that easily accessible for the academic researchers. Canada was behind by about a decade in its efforts at deregulation. In many ways, the Canadian experience is similar to that of Australia. Sinha (1993) compares the experience of Canada with Australia.

One of the early works is by Jordan (1986) who compares the effects of deregulation in the US with the regulated environment in Canada. His results showed that compared with Canada, airline deregulation in the US had many beneficial effects. These included a fall in average fares, a reduction in operating expenses, an increase in employee productivity, an increase in the number of air carriers, no overall effect on total employment in the industry, a reduction in the concentration of passenger traffic and a fall in the costs of strikes and lockouts.

One of the most comprehensive early studies about the effects of airline deregulation in Canada is by Oum, Stanbury and Tretheway (1991). The early effects of airline deregulation in Canada were as follows according to Oum, Stanbury and Tretheway. First, early evidence from deregulation in Canada suggests that the average yield per passenger mile in constant dollars fell after the two bouts of deregulation in 1984 and in 1988. At least, a part of it can be attributed to deregulation. As in the US, the percentage of travellers using discount fares increased. Second, service quality has a number of dimensions: flight frequency, the types of aircraft (jet aircraft are generally thought to be superior because of more legroom, higher quality of in-flight service, more comfortable feeling because of the adequate air pressure inside and so on), airline safety, in-time service, direct flights and the number of connections needed to reach the final destinations and a whole host of other factors. There was a substantial increase in the total number of flights during the early years of deregulation in Canada and this included services in the south as well as in the north and jet and non-jet services. However, jet services as a percentage of total departures fell as the airlines now rationalised their services and were using smaller aircraft in many cases. So, there might have been a fall in the quality of service in one dimension. However, the other dimension of quality has to do with intra-line versus interline transfers. Consumers prefer intra-line service i.e., a service where they do not have to change airline when they change planes to reach their destinations. As in the US case, the air travellers in Canada have also been able to increasingly use the intra-line transfers after deregulation. Finally, hub and spoke operations have been a feature associated with airline deregulation in the US. In Canada, this system did not develop fully because Canadian airline markets are not large enough for effective hub and spoke operations. This is similar to the experience in Australia as well.

Canada has a near duopoly situation in the domestic airline market. Air Canada and Canadian Airlines International and their subsidiaries have got the bulk of the passengers. The subsidiaries of these two airlines are as follows: Air BC, Air Ontario, Air Alliance, Air Nova and Canadian Regional. These airlines provide regional domestic and transborder services. There is substantial competition among the subsidiaries. The other group of independent airlines providing inter-regional, transcontinental, transborder and international services include the following: Air Transat, Canada 3000, Royal Airlines, SkyService, Westjet and First Air.

Figure 4.3 gives the number of air passengers from 1980 to 1998 (in thousands) in three categories – domestic, transborder and other international. Canada's close proximity to the United States means that the transborder passengers remain significant. In fact, the number of transborder passengers exceeds the number of other international passengers. The major Canadian cities are all within a distance of 200 miles of the Canadian borders. The ultimate destination of a very high percentage of international passengers is the United States. But, in addition, the close proximity of the United States means that United States remains the gateway for Canadian passengers for travelling to other parts of the world.

Airline safety had been always been a concern and used as an argument for regulation of airlines. However, as we will see, in the US case, the concern was unfounded because if anything, there is evidence that air travel has become safer after deregulation. Results from Canada show similar decreases in airline fatalities after deregulation.

Airline Regulation and Deregulation in Canada

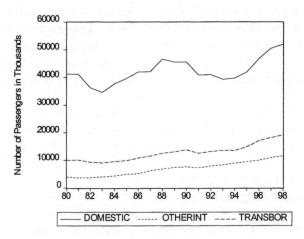

**Figure 4.3 Number of Domestic, Transborder and International
Passengers (in thousands), 1980-98**
Source: Transport Canada website (2000)

A three-year open skies agreement between Canada and the US was
signed in February 1995.   This is known as the new Air Services
Agreement (ASA) between the two countries. The ASA allowed freedom
of entry and pricing in transbroder markets. This has resulted in a 37%
increase in the transborder air traffic between the two countries. However,
the distribution of gains have not been shared equally by the airlines in the
two countries.   Out of every three additional passengers, two had been
carried by Canadian carriers and one had been carried by American carriers
(Flint, 1998).   For Air Canada, the flights to/from US account for one-
quarter of the total revenue and the routes and the yields are the highest on
these routes. The composition of traffic has also changed. Air Canada is
carrying more business travellers and less leisure travellers in these
transborder routes. Air Canada also has a code-sharing agreement with the
United Airlines (Star alliance).   Similarly, Canadian Airlines has also
benefited from the open skies policy.   Before the agreement, Canadian
Airlines served only three routes to/from US. Now, it serves 12.

During the early 1990s, both Air Canada and Canadian Airlines
International (CAI) incurred heavy losses partially because of competition
between two carriers and also because of the competition the carriers faced
from large US carriers. A proposal for mergers was mooted in 1992.
However, it failed to materialise.   However, in December 1999, the

61

Minister of Transport David Collenette approved Air Canada's proposed acquisition of Canadian Airlines International. The proposed arrangement is that for the time being, both airlines will continue to operate under their own names. CAI now becomes a subsidiary of Air Canada. The consolidation came in the wake of a hostile take-over bid of Air Canada by American Airlines and Onex Corporation.

The critics point out that the government has now created a near-monopoly in the provision of air passenger service. However, a number of conditions have been put on Air Canada to ensure fair pricing and the chance for other airlines to compete (Anonymous, 2000d). First, airline prices will be monitored by the government to prevent price gouging. Second, Canadian Regional Airlines, which is a subsidiary of Air Canada, must be put up for sale. Third, no involuntary layoffs or relocations of the unionised employees of the two airlines and their subsidiaries will be permitted. Fourth, the two airlines and their subsidiaries must continue to provide services to domestic city-pair markets that they were serving before the acquisition. Air Canada has to give up a number of peak-traffic landing slots at Toronto's Pearson international airport.

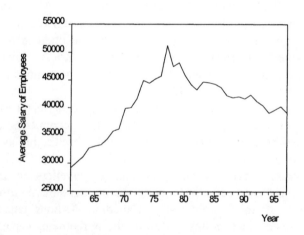

Figure 4.4 Average Salary of Employees in the Airline Industry, 1961-97

Source: Transport Canada website (2000)

Figure 4.4 shows the average salary of the employees in the airline industry from 1961 to 1997 in 1992 Canadian dollars. The average salary rose fairly steadily from 1961 to 1979 reaching a peak of $51,271 in 1977. Since then, it has almost steadily fallen now reaching roughly the level it was in 1970. The start of the fall in the average salary coincides with airline deregulation in the United States and the movement towards deregulation in Canada.

It is expected that the productivity of the airline employees would increase over the years. If the productivity is measured by passenger-kilometres per employees, this seems to be the case indeed. Figure 4.5 shows the index of productivity of the airline employees with 1961 as the base year. The productivity of the airline employees has steadily increased from one in 1961 to 5.77 in 1997. Although we focus mainly on airline passengers, it can be noted that the increase in productivity is even higher for cargo as measured by tonne-kilometres per employee. The index increased from one to 6.80 during the same period.

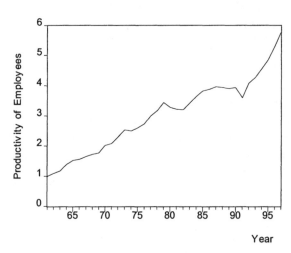

Figure 4.5 Index of Productivity of Employees in the Airline Industry, 1961-97

Source: Transport Canada website (2000)

We also expect that as the productivity of labour increases, labour cost as a percentage of operating costs will fall. As figure 4.6 shows, labour cost as a percentage of operating cost has fallen. In 1961, the share was 39.7 percent. In 1997, the share fell to 24.1 percent.

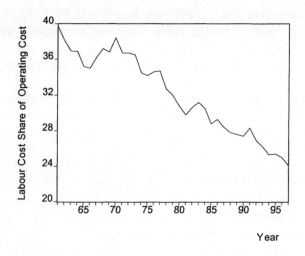

Figure 4.6 Labour Cost Share of Operating Cost in the Airline Industry, 1961-97

Source: Transport Canada website (2000)

Thus, labour efficiency has clearly increased. However, the same cannot be said about fuel efficiency. Fuel cost as a percentage of operating costs did not fall. It was 15 percent in 1955. It reached its peak of 25.3 in 1981. In 1997, it was 15.4 percent. However, fuel prices are, for the most part, beyond the control of the airlines. A better measure of fuel efficiency is the index of passenger kilometres per litre of fuel. Figure 4.7 shows an index of the fuel efficiency as measured by passenger-kilometres per litre of fuel (base 1981=1). It indicates a significant increase in fuel efficiency. The index increased from 0.56 in 1961 to 1.41 in 1997. Figure 4.8 shows the load factor for the major airlines in Canada. The load factor has been on an upward trend since the mid 1990s. However, more recent data for 1999 and 2000 for the two major airlines in Canada – Air Canada and CAIL – show a fall in the load factor. For both Air Canada and CAIL, the load factor plummeted to close to 60 percent in early 2000 (not shown in the figure).

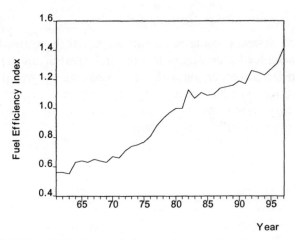

Figure 4.7 Fuel Efficiency Index of the Airline Industry, 1961-97
Source: Transport Canada website (2000)

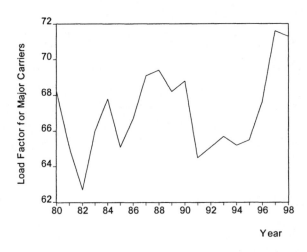

Figure 4.8 Load Factor for Major Air Carriers, 1980-98
Source: Transport Canada website (2000)

Conclusions

Unlike the United States, Canada has achieved partial deregulation. The results have been somewhat similar to that of the United States. However, as pointed out earlier, a comparison with the United States is fraught with a number of difficulties. In addition, the very large percentage of transborder passengers and close proximity of the major cities to the United States makes it hard to study the effects in isolation.

Chapter 5

Regulation and Liberalisation of Airlines in Europe

Introduction

There is no doubt that the regulatory reforms in air transportation in the US, Canada, New Zealand and other countries have influenced the thinking of the policy makers in Europe. Europe has been a relatively late starter in liberalising its air transportation. Even though Western European countries have moved towards substantial liberalisation in this regard during the later half of the 1990s, opinions among European governments remain divided. The legislation towards deregulation has been mooted mostly by dominant countries in the European Union.

Briand and Kelvin (1998) discuss a number of features of the European airline markets. Worldwide, there are 1,012 airports, which are accessible to the international traffic. Europe has 380 airports. United Kingdom, France, Germany, Netherlands and Italy accounted for over 25 percent of the world total passenger traffic in 1996. However, in 1978, the percentage was higher at 30.7 percent. Three European airlines, namely, Lufthansa, British Airways and Air France have been in the top ten airlines in the world. Competition has taken its toll on some of the European airlines. Air Europe (UK), Air Holland (Netherlands), EAS (France), Sterling Airways (Denmark) have failed in recent years. Other airlines such as Olympia Airways, Alitalia and Sabena are experiencing chronic deficits.

Figure 5.1 shows the number of domestic and international passengers in the European Union countries for 1970 to 1998. The number has almost steadily increased from 38 million in 1970 to 209 million in 1998.

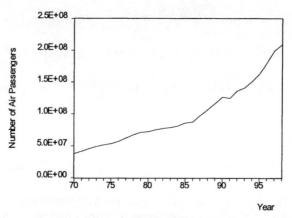

Figure 5.1 Number of Domestic and International Air Passengers in the European Union, 1970-98

Source: World Bank (2000)

Regulation of Airlines and its Consequences

The Chicago Convention in 1944 discouraged competition in the airline industry in Europe. Most countries in Europe had only one airline. In fact, the Chicago Convention led to the adoption of a general policy that a country would have only one airline. Price competition was almost non-existent as the airlines agreed on capacity in various routes. The system that resulted was characterised by low productivity, high per unit costs and high fares. Barrett (2000) discusses a number of effects of the Chicago Convention on European airports. First, the ban on new airlines led to lack of innovation in route development and the absence of low-cost non-colluding airlines. Second, the ban on price competition prevented low-cost airports to offer cheaper fares. Third, the arrangement of market sharing led to the practice of interchangeable tickets and concentration of airlines at hub airports. Fourth, grandfather rights to slots enabled airlines with slots at hub airports to concentrate on hubs. This eroded the authority of the airport management and led to an increase in the asset value of the slots. Finally, competition and efficiency were undermined. This resulted in weak airport management structure because of the lack of independent corporate airport structure.

The European Economic Community established a Common Transport Policy when it was formed in 1957. However, aviation was excluded from the Policy (Button, 1997). Even though the recent spate of liberalisation has produced a number of changes, it is unlikely that the European Union (EU) will ever have a deregulated aviation market as created by the Airline Deregulation Act of 1978 in the US. The EU's official preferred policy may not be the preferred policy of some of the member countries and a compromise is necessary in many cases. The Chicago Convention of 1944 failed to produce a global multilateral arrangement in aviation and bilateral agreements became common in Europe. But these bilateral agreements often did not permit fifth freedom.

Differences between the US and European Airline Markets

While the US is a single country with a huge domestic airline market (by far, the largest in the world), the European market is segmented because of the vast number of relatively small number of countries that comprise Europe. Good, Roller and Sickles (1993) and Button and Johnson (1998) provide a number of contrasting features of the US and EU airline markets. First, the US liberalised mainly its domestic market. In contrast, the EU market is mostly international. In 1990, 15.4 percent of departures and 8.9 percent of the passengers carried by the US carriers were international. The corresponding figures for EU registered carriers were 52.9 percent and 55.0 percent respectively. Since international markets are more regulated, the EU carriers have been able to extract more rent.

Second, historically speaking, the charter market has been much larger in the EU. In 1985, only 3 million of the 336 million domestic passengers in USA used charter services. In contrast, 42 million of the 162 million passengers within the member countries of European Civil Aviation Association used charter services during the same year. In the early 1990s, in the US, the charter services accounted for less than two percent of all passenger miles. In contrast, in Europe, it was more than twenty-five percent. Charter services are less useful for the business travellers. In Europe, in those markets that are predominantly for leisure travel, scheduled services tend to be almost non-existent. The charter operators have experience and this can lead to a more efficient traffic mix in the post-deregulation period.

Third, the average length of haul is 1300 kilometres in the United States whereas it is only 750 kilometres in Europe. While Europe has a larger population than the US, the geographical area of Europe is much smaller than the US, thus, the average length of trips is much smaller and there is less scope in Europe for using a hub and spoke system, which has been an increasing feature in the United States. Indirect flights with cheaper fares offer effective competition to the direct flights with higher fares in the United States. However, the same is not true in the EU countries.

Fourth, the size of the US airline market is much larger. Even though British Airways is, by far, the largest airline in the EU and has a very large market share, its size is quite small compared with that of the United Airlines or the American Airlines. The presence of an airline such as British Airways with a huge chunk of the market share in the EU can hinder entry.

Fifth, in the US, the airlines are privately owned and a number of airlines had to go out of business in the years following deregulation. In contrast, there is a substantial public sector participation in the ownership of airlines in the EU countries. Air France, Aer Lingus (Ireland), Iberia (Spain), Olympic (Greece) and TAP (Portugal) are owned fully by the governments. For many other airlines, the governments of the countries hold the majority of the shares. Government ownership can affect conduct since it is almost impossible for these airlines to go bankrupt. Government -owned airlines have to abide by the rules and regulations laid by the respective governments although these airlines clearly operate on a commercial basis and not as government departments. Still, the ownership issue is important in matters of regulation. The restructuring process that needs to happen in the case of government owned airlines is much more pronounced than the process to be undergone by the privately owned airlines under the process of liberalisation. Of course, the ultimate goal of many of the European countries is to privatise the airlines.

Sixth, except for the northeastern part, train services hardly offer any intermodal competition to air passenger transportation in the United States. In the US, train services have lost popularity over the years. One of the factors has been the cheap price of gasoline and therefore, the popularity of driving. In Europe, high-speed train services offer an effective competition to the airlines for passenger transportation. Train services, unlike the US but like Japan have remained very popular.

Seventh, Graham (1997b) points out a very important distinction between the European markets and the American markets. The nature of the European markets is such that it would be impossible to replicate the experience of the US. There is a limit beyond which the European liberalisation process simply cannot go. In the words of Graham (1997b, p. 807):

> In effect, no incumbent carrier of any substance can replicate another route structure; no market entrant can emulate the network of a major incumbent. The inevitable legacy of these processes is the concentration of a large number of carriers and hub airports in a relatively confined geographical area. The 17 EEA states support 15 national airlines, sometimes referred to as 'flag carriers'.

Finally, the timing of deregulation is also important. The Airline Deregulation Act was passed way back in 1978 in the United States. At that time, international air transportation was highly regulated. The changes in the EU are taking place at a time when international airline market is also being liberalised.

Liberalisation of Airline Service

We will deal mainly with Western Europe here. By Western Europe, we will mean the seventeen states of the European Economic Area (EEA). The most profitable routes for these airlines are not the intra-European flights but the inter-European flights.

Compared with the voluminous studies that have been done with respect to deregulation in the U. S., the works on the European deregulation remain meagre. In the context of Europe, the term 'liberalisation' rather than the term 'deregulation' is the term that is used. The multitude of countries can make access to data relatively more difficult. US was and remains so the place in which different theories of regulation were and are being tested. In contrast, the institutional structure of Europe hardly presents such an opportunity.

Phases of Liberalisation

The liberalisation process in Europe is hampered by the fact that there are so many countries and governments with different ideas so that it is difficult for them to agree on the optimal amount of deregulation. 21 different air control systems and 26 computer programming languages are used. French and south European governments were in favour of a restricted regime, whereas UK and Dutch were in favour of a rapid change towards deregulation. One reason for the United Kingdom and Netherlands to be in favour of more liberalisation is that these countries are fairly confined within their national boundaries.

The commentators emphasise the evolutionary nature of the process of liberalisation in Europe and contrast it with the one-step deregulation of the airlines in the US – the step being the passage of the Airline Deregulation Act of 1978. This is not entirely accurate. The process of deregulation in the US went through a number of stages as well. However, the process in Europe has been more long drawn.

As pointed out by Graham (1997b), historically speaking, the basic structure in Europe is that there are a number of discrete national networks that operate the major airlines. With the exception of Germany, the national capitals serve as the hubs for these airlines.

The Civil Aviation Memorandum Number 1 was published as early as 1979 by the European Commission. The memorandum recommended liberalisation of the aviation market in Europe. The recommendations included the need for airlines to offer cheaper fares, a more open access to markets and a universal policy towards subsidies. However, as Taneja (1988) notes, the dominant European countries were generally against these liberalisation policies. These countries subsidised their national carriers. These subsidies were for various purposes. These included the compensation of the operating loss of the airlines, provision of service to economically underdeveloped regions and the encouragement of the acquisition of specific aeroplanes.

The deregulatory process in Western Europe started with the ruling of the European Court of Justice in April 1986. The Court ruled that the air transportation would henceforward be subject to the competitive rules as proposed in the Treaty of Rome. The first phase of liberalisation started in December 1987 when the Council of Ministers adopted a number of measures aimed at opening market access, relaxing price controls and introducing new competition rules (Roller and Sickles, 1993). The first package came into effect from 1 January 1988. The second package was implemented from 1 November 1990. The implementation of the third package started from 1 January 1993 and ended on 1 April 1997. Graham (1997a) summarises the three phases as given in table 5.1.

Table 5.1 Air Transport Liberalisation Packages

1. Implemented from 1 January 1988	Allowed multiple designation, fifth-freedom rights, automatic approval of discount fares
2. Implemented from 1 November 1990	Double disapproval rule applied to full fares
3. Implemented from 1 January 1993; Final Implementation, 1 April 1997	No restrictions on pricing on all fares Full access to all routes including cabotage
	Abandonment of distinction between charter and scheduled carriers
	Protection for routes designated as public service obligations
	EC retention of right to intervene against fares, predatory pricing and seat dumping

Source: Graham (1997a)

Among the three different packages, the third package is the most important one. By April 1997, all EEA carriers gained access to all routes within the EC. The implementation of full cabotage implies the carriers are free to operate domestic services in any country irrespective of wherever their bases might be. Also, the third package abolished the distinction between scheduled and charter services. As noted earlier, chartered services are much more important in the context of Europe than in the case of the US. The charter services could now designate their flights as scheduled.

Captain and Sickles (1997) discuss the main aspects of the packages, especially that of the third package. Outlined below are the five most important aspects.

Fares: Airlines are generally free to choose their own fares. However, if there are complaints from national aviation authorities about excessive prices being charged, Brussels can intervene. Similarly, Brussels is authorised to prevent predatory pricing. In case of excessive price wars resulting in losses for all carriers, Brussels can set minimum fares.

Europe has followed a similar kind of policy with regard to fares as the US. The successive aviation packages have allowed discounting of fares. The first package allowed a discount of up to 55 percent. The second one allowed a discount of up to 70 percent. The double-disapproval mechanism was also introduced with the second phase. A fare would be permitted unless the governments in the origin and destination countries do not agree with such a fare and give reasons for such disagreement within 30 days of the publication of that fare. The third package allowed complete flexibility of fares subject to the double-disapproval mechanism of the second package. Even though Europe has gone through these packages with regard to fares, the fares per mile has remained rather high. In the US, the fares fell quickly after the implementation of the ADA Act.

Routes: Carriers are now allowed to add a domestic leg for a flight originating from the carrier's home base to a destination in another country provided the load factor on the domestic leg does not exceed 50 percent of the total of the main flight.

Flights: Airlines can now fly from their home bases to another country, pick up passengers and then continue on to another country without coming back to its home base. It can also have both origins and destinations in other countries. This is the sixth freedom under the Chicago convention.

Domestic services: Any carrier in any of the 12 EU countries can operate internal flights in any of the 12 EU countries effective April 1, 1997.

Licensing: New entrants are also subject to the common rules about financial requirements on capital adequacy and safety.

Since the liberalisation process began, only one carrier, namely British Airways, has been fully privatised. Governments have continued to subsidise the airlines thus inhibiting competition. The continuous infusion of state subsidy has prevented the achievement of the 'level-playing field' which is a goal of the liberalisation process. As the Civil Aviation Authority (1995) points out, the potential privately owned entrants have been the losers of such subsidies.

The third package applies mainly to air services within the European Union. However, the Commission is scheduled to extend it to Switzerland, Eastern Europe and some Mediterranean countries during the next few years (Humphreys, 1996).

74

The Effects of the Packages of Liberalisation

As pointed out earlier, there is a paucity of studies, which look at the effects of these three packages of liberalisation. Also, the benefits of the liberalisation are being realised slowly. The regulatory agencies such as Civil Aviation Authority in the UK have stressed that the primary beneficiaries have been the consumers (Graham, 1997b).

The theory of contestable markets can provide an analytical framework in judging the benefits from such liberalisation. We can distinguish between the effects of actual competition and potential competition. One version of the contestability theory says that if perfect contestability holds, potential competition has the same effect as actual competition. In the context of the United States, Morrison and Winston (1986) find that actual competition was three times more effective than potential competition. For Europe, one study (Civil Aviation Authority, 1995) finds that consumers gained only in those cases where there were at least three competitors in head-to-head competition. The gains to the consumers were in the form of lower prices, better service and better connecting flights.

Just as deregulation in the United States was marked by entry of low cost airlines, it has happened in Europe as well. Liberalisation has been followed by entry of no-frills airlines such as EasyJet, Ryanair and Virgin Express.

Even though the European markets are now much more deregulated, there are enormous differences in the productivity of the relatively more deregulated markets and the relatively less deregulated markets. Barrett (1999) compares the productivity of the routes between Ireland and UK and that of other 14 member airlines in the Association of European Airlines to find that fares had fallen much faster in the routes between Ireland and UK. The number of passengers per airline staff was found to be 4800 for Ryanair (serving the routes between UK and Ireland) compared with an average of 752 for the members of the Association in 1998. Ryanair has been able to reduce costs by slashing the travel agent commissions and by selling more and more tickets through telemarketing.

Labour cost accounts for between 25 percent to 33 percent of total cost of airlines. Deregulation has been accompanied by cost cutting by the airlines. One of the most important areas of cost cutting for airlines has been in the area of labour cost. Most studies on the United States find a substantial reduction in labour costs following deregulation. Alamdari and Morrell (1997) compare the experience of labour cost cutting per unit of output after deregulation in the United States and Europe. It is easier to cut labour costs during recessions. The initial years after deregulation in the United States were not followed by a recession – this made reductions in labour costs difficult. During the first four years after deregulation in the US, unit labour costs fell in real terms by about 10 percent mainly because of the decrease in wages rather than an increase in productivity. However, during the next four years when the recession had set in, there was a 17 percent fall in unit labour costs mainly because of the increase in productivity. In recent years, the increase in productivity has been accompanied by an increase in real wages. Unit labour costs fell in Europe as well after the recession. During the four-year period from 1991 to 1994, unit labour costs fell almost 23 percent as a result of the increase in productivity. The period was marked also by an increase in real wages.

Button (1996) discusses an important problem with regard to the European airline liberalisation – the issue of stability. A number of airlines especially in the US faced financial difficulties. These difficulties raise the fundamental question whether competition is sustainable or not. The theory of the core says that competition can often be unstable and inefficient. The problem of empty core arises when the industry's unit cost is not a non-increasing function of the industry's output. The presence of an empty core means that it would be beneficial for suppliers and users to form coalitions.

Humphreys (1996) tries to measure the effectiveness of liberalisation on the intra-European routes. The entry of a third carrier was found generally to increase service quality and lower price.

Barrett (2000) points out that one effect of airline deregulation has been to increase competition among airports. Low-cost airlines have a preference for newly privatised airports since these airports offer a large discount to these airlines. Air travellers also benefit from the lower airfares. Barrrett finds that underused airports showed a tremendous jump in passenger traffic when they were served by a low cost airline. There seems to be a huge scope of increasing traffic at many underused airports.

Good, Roller and Sickles (1993) point out that bilateral agreements have hindered the European networks of airline markets. These agreements specify the gateway cities (the cities which will be served) and the number of airlines that can serve these cities. In practice, in most cases, only one airline is specified by one country. Each country also specifies the right to carry passengers between two foreign countries. In contrast, in the US, the hub and spoke networks developed relatively quickly after the passage of the Airline Deregulation Act.

As noted before, historically speaking, airfares have been higher in Europe than in many other parts of the world, especially the US. Taneja (1988) finds a number of reasons for the higher airfares in Europe. First, the governments in the European countries often protect the inefficient carriers by providing subsidies and other benefits. Second, there is evidence of a high degree of cross subsidy among different routes. Thus, fares charged on unprofitable routes are often kept artificially low and thus, more dense city-pair markets cross-subsidise these routes. Third, the government policies lead to excessive profits for the airlines.

In Taneja's opinion, we cannot expect the fares in Europe to come down to the levels in the US even after a thorough liberalisation of the air transportation industry. Taneja attributes it to the differences in cost structures – the average cost per mile in Europe is higher than in the US. However, this explanation is only partially valid. The cost structure in Europe, to a certain extent, is a function of the inefficiencies caused by the regulation. As many of the inefficiencies of these regulations have now been removed, the cost structures of the airlines in Europe are bound to change. Only if the level of regulation and other things are similar, we can compare the cost structures of the airline industries in the two regions. However, as pointed out earlier, the average length of the flight is lower in Europe than in the US. This can still account for the differences in the cost structures in the two countries even after all regulations in Europe are removed.

Is Gradual Change a Better Strategy?

A number of authors have compared the experience of Europe with that of the US with regard to the pace of deregulation. The commission of the European Communities (1996) argues that the European Union has been able to reap the benefits of deregulation without the major upheavals seen in the case of the United States where a number of airlines had to exit. In other words, European countries have been able to reap the benefits without any major costs by following a policy of gradualism rather than a 'big bang' which is sometimes said to be characteristic of the changes in the airline market in the United States. However, Button and Johnson (1998) point out, such generalisations do not capture some of the things that happened.

There were elements of the changes in the United States which are not of the 'big bang' type. The Essential Air Service Act, which is still in operation, is an example of that. In addition, the European gradualism might have resulted in fewer benefits to the consumers.

Liberalisation in Eastern Europe

The trend towards liberalisation has also spread to eastern European countries and the ex-states of the USSR. Shibata (1994) offers three reasons for such a trend. First, it is hard for these new countries to provide foreign currency that is required for continuous fleet renewal. At the same time, the sale of airlines is a very quick way of generating cash. Second, the Western European countries have opened up their markets and it is now easier to attract foreign companies, which are too willing to enter Eastern European countries' airline markets. Third, the institutional changes that are taking place in Western Europe (such as privatisation of airlines) have affected Eastern European countries as well.

However, privatisation can mean many things in the context of the former Communist countries. While the government agencies are no longer able to provide an elaborate amount of control over airlines and airline operations, no alternative system is in place. In other words, as in many other fields in these countries, a vacuum has been created and no definite deregulatory policy is in place. Even though in many cases, there are no more controls over fares and prices of jet fuels, these cannot be attributed to deregulation.

In most cases, however, the erstwhile state-owned airlines have not been fully privatised. Instead, these airlines have acquired foreign partners. This arrangement has offered the foreign partners a newly opened market. In return, the eastern European airlines expect new injections of capital and technical know-how (Shibata, 1994).

Conclusions

Despite the fact that substantial liberalisation has taken place in Europe, most intra-European markets continue to be served by only two-flag carriers suggesting that duopoly has not been broken by liberalisation. As pointed out earlier, a comparison of the US market with the European market is fraught with a number of difficulties. However, comparisons about the effects of airline deregulation in the United States and liberalisation in Europe are often been made. Most studies find that the benefit to the consumers has been higher in USA than in Europe.

Chapter 6

Evolution of Regulation and Deregulation of Airlines in the US

Introduction

Comprehensive economic regulation of airlines in the United States began with the passage of the Civil Aeronautics Act of 1938. Over the years, minor changes were made to the regulatory framework but the basic statute remained intact throughout the period of regulation. The 1970s saw increasing dissatisfaction with the working of the regulatory framework in various fields in the US and regulatory reforms swept the airline, railroad, trucking, financial and, telecommunications industries. The central theme of this chapter is that although the federal government introduced airline regulation to promote consumer or public interest, over time regulation tended to promote the interests of the airline industry rather than those of the public.

It will be argued in this chapter that the public interest theory provided the rationale for regulating the airlines, especially after the submission of the Federal Aviation Commission Report in 1935. The legislations during the late 1920s and early 1930s were aimed at fixing the problems at hand and were piecemeal in nature. Some economists argued that without regulation, there would be "excessive competition" in the airline industry. There would be chaos and the service to passengers and freight would suffer. However, excessive competition was never clearly defined. The US government was convinced that only a regulated airline industry would provide safe and adequate service. The government was in favour of regulated competition to promote public interest. This philosophy of the government became especially clear after the establishment of the Civil Aeronautics Board (CAB) in 1938. In many ways, the CAB's role with respect to airlines was the same as that of the Interstate Commerce

Commission with respect to railroads and trucking. The government's justification for the existence of the two bodies was virtually similar.

Subsequently, many analysts argued that airline regulation did not promote the public interest because the airline industry was inherently competitive in nature. Some economists found evidence that although the federal government introduced regulation to promote public interest, airlines formed an imperfect cartel and enjoyed monopoly. Thus, these economists found evidence of the capture theory.

Theories of Regulation

There are two basic theories of regulation: the public interest theory of regulation and the economic theory of regulation. We discuss the two theories briefly.

The Public Interest Theory of Regulation

The origin of this theory goes back to the days of the case of Munn vs. Illinois. This was when the legal concept of regulation applying to "businesses affected with the public interest" was introduced. The public interest concept had a tremendous influence on the legislators, the decision of commissioners and scholars for a long time after that. The policy of New Deal was influenced by the public interest concept and so were the establishments of Interstate Commerce Commission and the Civil Aeronautics Board.

Public interest can be defined in utilitarian terms. Zerbe and Urban (1988) give a simple example which uses Kaldor-Hicks test with appropriate adjustment for distributional effects (following Harberger, 1978). Table 6.1 shows the benefits and costs of Project A.

Table 6.1 Benefits and Costs of Project A

	Poor	Rich	Opportunity Cost Adjustment	Total
Costs	$-100	$-100	$---	$-200
Benefits	150	50	---	200
Unadjusted Net Benefits	50	-50	---	0
Adjusted Net Benefits	50	-50	12.5	12.5

Source: Zerbe and Urban (1988)

The assumption here is that the cost of the most efficient method of transferring wealth to the poor is 25 percent of the amount transferred. Thus, an expenditure of $62.50 has to be incurred to transfer $50 to the poor. Therefore, the net benefit of the project is $12.50. The distributionally adjusted net benefits measure the public interest element. If this measure is positive (as in this hypothetical example), we can say that regulation is in the public interest.

The public interest theory of regulation stresses the role of market failures. These market failures can take various forms. Armstrong, Cowan and Vickers (1994) for example, divide the market failures into the following three categories.

Asymmetric Information We can discuss the asymmetric information from the consumer's point of view and from the regulator's point of view. From the consumer's point of view, a market failure takes place when the consumer does not have complete information or cannot judge the quality of the product given the available information. Regulatory agencies can help consumers to decide in such cases because they can provide consumers with the knowledge. While for some products like drugs, consumers may need such information, for other products, it may be sufficient for the consumers to have warranties for products.

Asymmetric information can also exist at the regulatory level. Generally, it is assumed that the regulator has all the relevant information. The regulator needs the information so that she/he can analyse the information and take regulatory measures, which protect the consumers. The regulator must be able to collect the relevant information at a reasonable cost.

Externalities Externalities, especially negative externalities, are considered to be important reasons for market failures. The concern for pollution is one of the most important reasons for the support of regulation.

Market Power As it is well known, monopoly is not conducive to the achievement of productive and allocative efficiencies. Monopoly power in cases of duopolies and oligopolies can also lead to barriers to entry resulting in concentration and inefficiency.

The natural monopoly argument has been used as a justification of regulation. Whereas under perfectly competitive market, producers produce up to the point where price is equal to marginal cost, the monopolist can have a lower output since the monopolist can raise market price by lowering output.

Now, we look at the institutional variant of the public interest model, which has been summarised by Trebing (1987). This variant is based on five major postulates. First, industrial societies give rise to concentrations of power, increased uncertainty, performance failures, uncompensated costs, and adverse distributional effects. Government regulation is called for to correct these malfunctions. Second, monetary or market oriented measures cannot promote social values optimally. Thus, government intervention is needed. Third, appropriate regulation can lead to higher levels of efficiency and greater individual choice. Fourth, the success of regulation in promoting public interest depends upon a popular consensus regarding the need for action and political support for the regulator. Fifth, the form of regulation may change over time because the regulatory process is evolutionary.

A theory related to the public interest theory is the positive institutional theory of regulation (Majone, 1996). Even though some of the elements of the institutional theory of regulation have become part of the public interest theory of regulation, some other institutionalists have developed a separate theory of regulation. Unlike the other two theories (the public interest theory and the economic theory of regulation) which were developed mostly by economists, the institutional theory was developed mostly by political scientists. This theory is to be distinguished from the institutional variant of the public interest theory. The basic premise of the positive institutional theory of regulation is that institutions are peripheral in the two main theories. The positive institutional theory of regulation draws on the works of public choice theorists, the new institutionalists and the economics of organisations. The theory therefore, looks at the political and bureaucratic linkages through which interests are translated into public policy.

The traditional or public interest theory of regulation reigned supreme for a long time. The theory has been referred to as the "normative-as-positive theory" by Joskow and Noll (1981). Apart from the market failures, the theory has also suggested that "destructive competition" or too much competition is not healthy either. For example, railroads in the United States came to be regulated in 1887 on the ground that there was destructive competition in the railroads.

The theory has come for criticisms from many economists. The earlier critics of the theory in the context of public utilities include Averch and Johnson (1962) in the context of the public utilities. They argue that cost-of-service regulation tends to distort input choices of the firm. In particular, it induces a firm to use too much capital to expand its rate base. The study by Averch and Johnson is a theoretical study, which has led to a number of empirical studies, which test the validity of the Averch-Johnson theory (also known as the A-J effect in the literature). Empirical studies have used mostly cross-section data on public utilities to study the effect. Joskow and Noll (1981) point out that the empirical studies on the subject are not conclusive.

There have been other strands of industrial organisation literature, which have challenged the public interest theory. The classic study by Stigler and Friedland (1962) find that regulation did not affect firm conduct. In the context of airlines, Caves (1962) finds that regulation did not eliminate but created inefficiencies.

Market power has been one of the most important reasons for regulation put forward by the public interest theory. However, some economists have argued that this is not a good enough reason for regulation. For example, in the context of electric utilities, Demsetz (1968) argues that proper pricing of the resources of the community will ensure efficiency. For electricity generation, if we have multiple providers, they will have the right to lay lines under the streets but they have to pay fees to the communities for using the streets. If the use of such common properties is efficient, the duplication of costs will not occur.

Economic Theory of Regulation

The self-interest theory of regulation or the economic theory of regulation (which is also known as the Chicago theory of regulation) was first proposed by Stigler (1971). While the public interest theory is a normative theory of regulation, the self-interest theory is a positive theory. Just like the public interest theory, this theory comes in many different forms. The main contribution of the theory is to incorporate political behaviour into the analysis. Just like other groups, politicians and regulators are interested in maximising their own utility. Thus, those groups that are affected by regulation can influence regulations by providing financial and other supports to the regulators and the politicians. Besides Stigler's pioneering contribution to the theory, Posner (1971), Peltzman (1976, 1989) and Becker (1983) have made important contributions to the theory.

Development of Regulation

Regularly scheduled air services in the U.S. were offered for the first time in 1918. Airmail service was inaugurated on May 15, 1918, on the New York-Philadelphia-Washington route using army equipment and personnel (Taneja, 1976). Vietor (1990, p. 6) observes:

> The airline business in America started out as a dangerous, heavily subsidized, mail delivery service. Government virtually created the market, long before the technology could sustain nation-wide passenger service.

The Post Office, through the development of airmail, was directly responsible for the beginning of commercial air transportation. Passenger service did not begin on a regular basis until 1925 when the Los Angeles-San Diego route was opened. It took one and one-half hours to fly

85

between Los Angeles and San Diego. The one way fare was $17.50 while the round trip was $26.

The production of aircraft jumped during the 19 months of the US's involvement in World War I. However, peace brought an end to this boom. Most of the contracts for manufacturing aeroplanes were cancelled and the size of the manufacturing side of the industry shrunk to about ten percent of what it was during the war. The transportation side of the business suffered even more. The safety record was not good. Instability and low public standing led to high insurance costs and a dearth of investment capital. By 1921, federal regulation of the airline industry came to be favoured by officials and civilian experts. This group persuasively argued for federal regulation to protect public interest.

Herbert Hoover who became Commerce Secretary in 1921 was a firm believer in the government sponsorship and regulation of commercial aviation. As Lee (1984, p. 92) notes:

> Hoover built a strong case for the government-sponsored development of commercial aviation. A thriving commercial aviation industry would help sustain in peacetime the manufacturing capability that would be needed in case of war and also provide a ready reserve of trained personnel and planes. Without commercial aviation, the government alone would have to bear the expense of maintaining an air capability probably through a subsidy program that Hoover considered unwise. Further, Hoover realised that faster transportation would bolster the national economy.

Hoover's ideas on how the industry should be regulated were heavily influenced by the industry experts. This was quite natural because the number of aviation experts was small in 1921.

The Senate Transportation Committee (as quoted in Taneja, 1976, p. 58) reported in 1921 about the introduction of legislation to regulate the industry:

> No one appeared or asked to have appeared in opposition to it. Representatives of the industry urged its passage and letters were received from many who could not come urging its passage.

To alleviate some of the problems faced by the industry, the first important act with regard to airlines, the Airmail Act (also known as the Kelly Mail

Act because representative Clyde Kelly of Pennsylvania sponsored the Act) was passed in 1925. It required that the award of airmail contracts be made by competitive bidding and provided subsidies for commercial airmail. The aim of this legislation was to encourage commercial aviation and to transfer airmail operations to private carriers. The federal government believed that development of commercial aviation was essential for a vast country like the USA. It was also thought that airmail operations could not be carried out more efficiently by the private sector at a lower cost. The subsidies led to heavy competition among the suppliers. However, competitive bidding limited profit for the carriers. Mail service mileage increased rapidly.

The period after 1925 was marked by fast growth in air passenger travel. "By 1930, passenger travel in the US nearly equalled total airline passenger travel in the rest of the world" (Taneja, 1976, p. 1).

Between 1918 and 1937, fifteen Congressional investigations were conducted in the field of aeronautics. The Air Commerce Act was passed in 1926. It was designed to encourage passenger services. The effect of the Kelly Act was that the carriers concentrated on airmail service and were not particularly interested in providing passenger services. The Air Commerce Act initiated the development of civil airways, navigational aids and provided for the regulation of safety by the federal government (Caves, 1962). The safety regulation included: the registration of aircraft; the rating of aircraft as to airworthiness; examination and rating of airmen; navigational facilities, and aviation schools; the rating of airlines and the establishment of air traffic rules. The Act also relieved the carriers of investing in what has come to be known as 'sunk costs' such as investment in ground facilities, as such costs were now to be borne by the federal government. The government was clearly guided by the idea of having a stable and viable airline industry. The Act was more promotional than regulatory in nature.

The Airmail Act of 1930 (McNary-Watres Act) was passed in April 1930. The main purpose of the act was to unify the industry. Walter Brown, the Postmaster General (PMG) initiated the Act. According to Brown, airlines were using obsolete aircraft, unable to pay sufficient attention to safety because of cost cutting necessitated by competitive bidding for airmail contracts and were unwilling to invest in new equipment. Brown believed that the airlines could develop without the airmail subsidy. He urged the airlines to develop their passenger service. He argued against the competitive bidding for airmail contracts. The Air Mail Act of 1930 gave the PMG wide ranging powers. The PMG could grant an airmail contract without competitive bidding. Under the Act, the mail payment rates were to be based on space instead of weight. Because of this change in the computation of mail payment rates, the airlines started acquiring larger planes. This gave a boost to passenger transportation. The airmail rates also took into account such variables as bad weather, bad terrain, night flying, radio equipment and multi-engine aircraft. Brown's vision of national air transportation was one in which there would be "regulated competition".   Brown believed that regulated competition would promote public interest in a better fashion than either monopoly or "excessive competition". Brown's tenure of four years as the PMG was marked by mergers and consolidation of airlines. Most of the larger airlines of today emerged during this period. Many smaller airlines ceased, as they could not secure mail contracts.

As noted earlier, the Post Office was responsible for the creation of commercial aviation in the US. However, it was recognised that Post Office airmail operation would be temporary in nature and would be turned over to private industry. In June 1927, the Post Office pilots were released as the newly formed airlines took over the airmail routes (Kane and Voss, 1977).

Extensive dissatisfaction among the public regarding the regulatory arrangements led to the passage of the Air Mail Act of 1934 (Black-McKeller Act). As Caves (1962, p. 123) observes:

> Earlier in 1934, the Postmaster General had cancelled all the existing contracts with airlines to carry air mail, on the basis of charges that they had originally been parcelled out in 1930 not according to proper competitive bidding but through a collusive spoils session.

The Air Mail Act was aimed at strengthening control of the air transportation industry. As was the case before 1930, the Post Office awarded airmail contracts through competitive bidding and enforcing airmail regulations. However, the three carriers, which were involved in the alleged collusion, were not given any contracts. These carriers were American Airways (which later changed its name to American Airlines), Eastern Air Transport (which later changed its name to Eastern Airlines) and Transcontinental Air. The Interstate Commerce Commission was to set 'fair and reasonable' rates of mail payments and to see that the payments were kept within the limits of anticipated postage earnings. The Interstate Commerce Commission was also given the responsibility of controlling entry. The Bureau of Air Commerce (predecessor of Federal Aviation Administration) in the Department of Commerce was to regulate safety in air transportation and was also responsible for airway maintenance and development. Another provision of the Act required separation of airline carriers and aircraft manufacturers. It was considered a matter of safety that aeroplane users not be controlled by the aeroplane builders. Had the same holding company been allowed to own an airline manufacturing concern, the airline might be required to buy an aeroplane from that manufacturing concern and so not necessarily choose the safest aircraft.

The Great Depression took its toll on the airline industry. After the resumption of competitive bidding for airmail contracts, the airlines, which previously got the bulk of the contracts, sought to regain them. Some airlines submitted very low bids. The incomes of several airlines fell dramatically. The entire airline industry was on the verge of a collapse in 1935. By this time, it was clear to the airlines that they could not depend on the airmail contracts for their survival, so they started to develop their passenger traffic. The major airlines opened their traffic and sales departments to promote and sell passenger travel. By December 1936, the income from passengers overtook the income from airmail services.

The arrangements under the 1934 Act did not work too well for two reasons. First, the distribution of responsibility among three agencies did not work satisfactorily. Second, the competitive bidding mechanism under the Act proved to be unworkable. For example, as mentioned earlier, carriers accused of collusion were forbidden from bidding; this caused many corporate carriers to change their names which allowed them to take part in the bidding.

During the period 1934-38, none of the agencies was satisfied with the existing arrangements. There was the problem of co-ordination among the agencies involved in regulation. In January 1935, the Federal Aviation Commission submitted its report after a thorough study of all aspects of aviation and after compiling an extensive record of testimony and statements. The Commission's main recommendations were the following. First, a comprehensive system of regulation was recommended. The jurisdiction over air carriers was to be given to a single authority. The Interstate Commerce Commission was overburdened and therefore ought not to be given it. The formation of a separate 'air commerce commission' for exercising regulatory powers was recommended. Second, the Commission felt that air transportation needed direct government aid to survive at this stage of development. Third, the Commission was in favour of a competitive organisation for the airline industry. It felt that there should be no arbitrary denial of the right of entry of newcomers into the field if they could adequately show that they were ready to render a better public service than could otherwise be obtained. The Commission observed that "present operators of airlines have no inherent right to a monopoly of the routes they serve" (*Report of the Federal Aviation Commission*, 1935, p. 61).

Fourth, although the Commission advocated competition, it believed that such competition should be controlled. It argued that excessive competition was as bad as too little. Excessive competition without any regulation was supposed to be in conflict with public interest for several reasons. It would lead to 'cream skimming' on the part of the operators, i.e., services to socially desirable but unprofitable routes would be discontinued. The Commission was in favour of cross-subsidising the low traffic volume routes with high volume traffic routes. If the traffic were sufficient to support only one carrier to provide high class service in a city-pair market, it would be unwise to allow more than one airline to operate in such a market. The Commission (*Report of the Federal Aviation Commission*, 1935, p. 63) observed:

> To allow half a dozen airlines to eke out a hand-to-mouth existence where there is enough traffic to support one really first-class one alone would be a piece of folly. To try to maintain a multiplicity of services in such a case by giving direct governmental aid would be the folly thrice compounded.

The Commission felt that unfettered competition would keep the industry in a state of flux with too many entries and exits, thus threatening the stability of the industry. The Commission recommended that no airline should be allowed to operate without obtaining a certificate of public convenience and necessity from the regulatory body. It was recommended that the regulatory authority be given control over accounts and reports, rates and fares, intercorporate relationships and financial structures.

President Roosevelt was initially opposed to the idea of a separate air commerce commission to being given the responsibility of regulating the airlines. Instead, he wanted the creation of a division in the Interstate Commerce Commission, which would have the exclusive task of dealing with regulation of air service. The Congress was in favour of creating a separate body and this led to an impasse. However, Roosevelt later gave in and withdrew his opposition.

More than three years of extensive discussion followed the presentation of the Report of the Federal Aviation Commission. The Civil Aeronautics Act was passed in 1938 after a long legislative history. This was the most important single piece of legislation in the history of airline regulation before the passage of the Airline Deregulation Act of 1978. Under this Act, various duties of economic regulation was assigned to the Civil Aeronautics Authority, the Civil Aeronautics Administration and the Air Safety Board. In 1940, some administrative changes were made. The Civil Aeronautics Board (CAB) was established as an independent agency to perform some of the functions of the Civil Aeronautics Administration and the Air Safety Board. The Air Safety Board was eliminated and the Administrator of Civil Aeronautics was transferred to the Department of Commerce. Thus, the CAB became virtually the sole agency in control of economic regulation.

The CAB was composed of five members appointed by the President of the United States, with the consent of the Senate for a term of six years. Not more than three out of five members could come from the same political party. As Richmond (1961) notes, the Board was given the responsibility of conducting the following activities: the control of entry of new carriers into the industry and entry of existing carriers into new or existing routes; the control of exit by requiring approval of the Board before a carrier's abandonment of service to a point or on the route; the regulation of fares on every route. It also fixed and awarded subsidies, controlled mergers, interlocking relationships and intercarrier agreements and eliminated rate discrimination and unfair competition or unfair and deceptive practices in air transportation.

Title I of the Civil Aeronautics Act of 1938 provided guidelines to the Board in carrying out its functions of economic regulation, stressing the public interest and 'public convenience and necessity'. It was to encourage and develop an air transportation system properly adapted to the present and future needs; regulate air transportation in such a manner as to recognise the inherent advantages of, assure the highest degree of safety in, and foster sound economic conditions in such transportation; promote adequate, economical, and efficient service by air carriers at reasonable charges without unjust discriminations, undue preferences or advantages, or unfair or destructive practices; promote, encourage and develop civil aeronautics.

The CAB was given the responsibility of achieving a number of objectives, some of which might be at cross-purposes with one another. For example, maximal contribution to the national defence might not lead to a policy, which achieved foreign and domestic needs optimally. Substantial discretion was, therefore, called for on the part of the Board. Titles IV and X of the Civil Aeronautics Act dealt with the detailed features of air carrier regulation. Section 401 set forth that no carrier should operate in interstate commerce without a certificate of public convenience and necessity.

Under the 'grandfather clause', sixteen carriers were granted certificates to provide air transportation service. The grandfather clause gave existing operators the certificates to operate after the passage of an Act routinely unless there were strong reasons for not granting such certificates. These carriers became known as the trunk airlines. When the certificates were being given under the grandfather clause for the scheduled services, a number of carriers were providing non-scheduled services. These carriers were exempt from obtaining certificates of public convenience and necessity but were to register themselves and furnish annual reports. The uncertificated carriers were later divided into two groups: the small irregular carriers (later to be known as air taxi operators and commuter carriers) and large, irregular carriers (later to be known as supplemental carriers). Sections 403 and 404 dealt with the subject matter of airfares and rates. According to Section 404, the carrier must establish and adhere to rates in such forms as the Board prescribed. Section 404 gave comprehensive authority to the Board to reject, modify, or revise any tariff. It could set exact fares, minimum or maximum limits, or both.

The framers of the Civil Aeronautics Act of 1938 were influenced by the public interest theory. It was believed that regulation was necessary to protect the public interest. There were criticisms from some analysts that the whole system of control of entry into the industry was unnecessary and unwise. However, the Federal Aviation Commission (*Report of the Federal Aviation Commission*, 1935, p. 52) said:

> There should be a certain measure of control by the government of the right of entry into the business in order that proper standards may be enforced and an irresponsible campaign of mutual destruction on the part of the operators avoided.

Public interest was the dominant criterion for the CAB in considering any application for new service. In a 1941 case, the CAB stated that four questions should be considered in any such application (Berge, 1955).

First, would the new service serve a useful public service, responsive to a public need? Second, could and would this service be served adequately by existing routes and carriers? Third, could the new service be served by the applicant without impairing the operation of existing carriers contrary to public interest? Fourth, would any cost of the proposed service to the government be outweighed by the benefit, which would accrue to the public from the new service?

The existing carriers were somewhat protected from new carriers because the new carriers had to produce the certificates of public convenience and necessity. While competition was recognised as an important force to be encouraged, excessive competition was believed to be destructive. Unfair or destructive competition used to be a very important part of the economists' language during the first half of the twentieth century. For example, Berge (1951, p. 7) observes:

> It is clear from this that our public policy favors competition with the exception of *unfair or destructive competitive practices*. Congress left it to the Board to determine the *extent* of competition necessary to assure the sound development of air transportation.

The airline network experienced rapid growth during the 1940s. The CAB allowed route expansion by domestic trunk airlines but tightly controlled mergers. The Civil Aeronautics Act disapproved mergers if they tended to create a monopoly and thereby restrained competition or jeopardised another carrier. In 1940, a merger between United and

Western was turned down on the grounds that the combined carrier would have offered east-west service from four major west-coast cities, whereas its competitors served only two such cities (Caves, 1962). In 1945, American Airlines was not allowed to acquire Mid-Continental Airlines on the ground that such a take-over would promote monopoly on certain routes (Civil Aeronautics Board, Docket 2068, 1946). In many cases, especially of mergers between local service carriers, the Board insisted that the carriers show that the mergers would be in the public interest. 'Route integration' (offering of significant new single-carrier service) and reduction in subsidy were accepted as promoters of public interest.

Airport development did not keep pace with the increasing traffic. The Civil Aeronautics Authority in its report recommended federal participation in the development of an adequate system of airports, including financial assistance (*Airport Survey*, 1945). The Federal Airport Act was passed in 1946. Before 1946, the airports were financed and operated by the state, county or municipal governments. These agencies were not able to cope with the increasing cost of building and maintaining airports. Under the Federal Airport Act, the task of building and maintaining airports fell on the Civil Aeronautics Administration. It was expected that small communities would benefit from the new arrangements.

During the late 1940s the financial stability of the airlines were of much concern to the Congress as financial losses of the carriers continued to mount. The Senate Committee on Interstate and Foreign Commerce held a series of hearings to investigate the issues. Two questions that were discussed thoroughly in these hearings were subsidy and competition. In 1938, the Congress authorised the payment of subsidies in the form of airmail payments to meet the legitimate financial needs of the certificated air carriers. Apart from the direct airmail subsidies, there were indirect airway and airport aids. These were justified on two grounds: infant industry argument and national defence. Many airline representatives appearing before the hearings complained that the CAB was too liberal in issuing certificates of public convenience and necessity (*Airline Industry Investigation*, 1947). The CAB Chairman denied the charge. He explained that the airlines would have charged CAB of stifling a dynamic industry if the CAB had been conservative in approving new routes and route extensions in the face of market expansion.

Some transportation analysts were, by then, urging caution against elaborate regulation of airline service. Berge (1951, pp. 8-9) observed:

Today public utility concept has become so broad as to practically defy clear definition. The term is used to cover a variety of unlike situations. Unfortunately, the indiscriminate use of the term public utility has led to the assumption that all so-called public utilities should be subjected to the same type of public regulation. Thus, not only railroads but also motor, water, and air carriers are loosely called public utilities despite vast differences between the economic characteristics of these transportation industries as compared with the typical characteristics of gas, electric power, and telephone utilities. ....It may be added that, while it requires more capital to engage in air transport than in motor transport, the amount in either case is minuscule as compared with that required to build a railroad or gas plant. Actually, it may be said that the only way to achieve conditions of monopoly in air transport is by closely restricting entry into the industry.

During the late 1930s and 1940s, the CAB was not paying enough attention to the problems of airline rate policy. Keyes (1951, p. 27) notes:

Although the Civil Aeronautics Board Act contains provisions for the regulation of commercial rates which are substantially similar to those applicable to surface carriers under the Interstate Commerce Act, the direct regulatory attainment of reasonable and non-discriminatory commercial rates was not conceived to be one of the primary tasks of the Civil Aeronautics Board, nor did it assume any great significance in the period immediately following the enactment of the law.

Also, according to Gill and Bates (1949), little attention was paid to cost factors in setting airline fares. There were two important reasons for this. First, neither the CAB nor the airlines had accurate figures for the cost of various types of passenger and cargo service. Second, unit cost of airlines being very high at that time, cost-based fares would have been prohibitively high from the standpoint of rail competition.

Even by 1955 (fifteen years after the establishment of the Civil Aeronautics Board), no new domestic trunk carriers were allowed to enter the airline industry. By then, thirteen new local service carriers had been certificated, but they accounted for only 2.3 percent of the industry's commercial revenues in 1954. To increase competition in the trunk routes, the CAB extended the routes of the grandfather carriers. However, by 1951, restraints on expansion of existing carriers' routes had been considerably tightened up. Some legal experts and economists were sharply critical of the Board's trunkline entry policies. Maclay and Burt (1955) have a thorough discussion of the Board's entry policy. Crane (1944) provides an even earlier critique.

The passage of the Civil Aeronautics Act of 1938 enormously increased the regulatory functions and responsibilities of the government. Additional legislation seemed to be needed to deal with various problems that cropped up as a result of the tremendous growth in domestic airline industry, which was partly due to the increased use of long-haul propeller aircraft in the late 1940s and 1950s. Under these circumstances, the Federal Aviation Act of 1958 was passed to amend the Civil Aeronautics Act of 1938. The new Act created a new agency named Federal Aviation Agency, which later came to be known as the Federal Aviation Administration (FAA). The FAA was made responsible for regulating air space; acquiring, operating and developing air navigation facilities and prescribing traffic rules for all aircraft. Air safety regulation was also the responsibility of the FAA. However, there was no change so far as economic regulation was concerned. The CAB continued to be in charge of economic regulation as well as of the investigation of civil aircraft accidents. The Act also made the CAB an independent agency. Previously, it was attached to the Department of Commerce.

Jet aircraft were being introduced during the late 1950s and, by the mid 1960s, at a very rapid pace. The introduction of jet aircraft changed the cost structure of the airlines. Although the initial investment for a jet plane was higher, the high productivity and prospective long life tended to reduce unit costs. However, Caves (1961) who analyses the cost structures of aircraft showed that there was a trade-off between higher speed and costs for newer aircraft (such as DC-7 and Lockheed-49). In order to set fares at levels which provided an appropriate return on investment for the airlines, the CAB initiated the General Passenger Fare Investigation (GPFI) in 1956, which was completed in 1960. A rate of return of 10.25 percent for the 'Big Four' (United Airlines, Eastern Airlines, Trans World Airlines and American Airlines) and 11.25 per cent for the other carriers were allowed by the CAB (Taneja, 1976). In setting these returns, the CAB employed the cost-of-capital technique. This methodology involves the separate determination of the cost of embedded debt capital, the appropriate rate of equity capital, determined by an inquiry into investor-earnings requirements and earnings on investment in comparable enterprises, and the appropriate capital structure, or percentage of debt and equity, which should be recognised in combining the costs of the two components into the overall rate of return. The CAB established a general policy of setting fare levels on the basis of cost of providing such service but it in practice, it was not followed in most cases. The economy and air traffic growth slowed down by the 1970s. Excess capacity of the carriers grew because the carriers had ordered new jet aircraft. In 1969, the Board approved rate increases in markets under 1800 miles as the industry's profits plummeted. Some other changes in the field of transportation also took place in the mid 1960s. The United States Department of Transportation (DOT) was created in 1966 to engage in research, planning and promotion of transportation and to regulate transportation safety.

One criticism about the setting of fares by the CAB had been that fares were not related to the cost of service. The CAB initiated the Domestic Passenger Fare Investigation (DPFI) in 1970 (Civil Aeronautics Board, 1976). The investigation examined aircraft depreciation, leased aircraft, deferred federal income taxes, joint fares, discount fares, seating configuration and load factor, fare level, rate of return, and fare structure. One of the major aims of this investigation was to establish fare levels, which generally reflected the cost of service. However, pursuant to the investigation, the CAB set fares almost solely on the basis of distance although distance was not clearly the only factor affecting cost of service. The Board established load factors and seating density standards, as well as a target rate of return.

The fares set by the DPFI bore more relationship to costs than before but the Board adopted the deliberate policy of setting fares above costs in markets of more than 400 miles and less than the costs in short-haul routes. This was done because of the economies of stage length, which meant that the unit costs were lower for long-haul markets than for the short-haul markets. If fares were set strictly on the basis of costs, passengers flying short distances would have paid a higher fare per mile. Route density clearly affects cost of service but was not taken into account. Peak-load pricing was not discussed very much. In fact, the carriers were discouraged from using off-peak fares on a greater scale on the grounds that it would be "confusing to the public and costly for the carriers to adminster". (Bailey, Graham and Kaplan, 1985, p. 20). Thus, even the DPFI did not satisfactorily take cost of service into account when setting fares.

Development of Deregulation

In the 1970s, some economists became increasingly vocal in their criticisms of the CAB regulation. The experience of the intrastate carriers, which were outside the jurisdiction of the CAB, provided additional incentives for deregulation. The studies by Douglas and Miller (1974), Jordan (1970), Kahn (1971), Keeler (1972), and Levine (1965), among others, were important in this respect. We look briefly at the studies of Jordan and Douglas and Miller. These were the two most important studies, which brought out the inefficiencies of regulation. Kahn, Keeler and Levine provide similar arguments in favour of deregulation.

The study by Jordan (1970) tries to bring out the inefficiencies of CAB regulation by comparing the performance of the California intrastate markets, which were subject to regulation by the California Public Utilities Commission, and other markets, which were regulated by the Board. From the very beginning, the Board's powers over the certificated carriers were in the field of entry, exit, routes served and fares. In California up to September 1965, the only regulation exercised by the California Public Utilities Commission was on the price charged by the intrastate or interstate scheduled carriers. Jordan finds no evidence that regulation protected the consumers.

Douglas and Miller (1974) develop a model of airline behaviour under economic regulation. Economic efficiency requires that service of given quality be produced at lowest feasible cost. It also requires prices (fares) to be equal to marginal cost and average cost and optimal price quality combinations be attained. But the authors' analysis show that airline fares were inefficient in the sense that resulting price-quality combinations were higher than those leading to cost minimisation of the travellers. The cost of service was affected in many ways by the Board's policies. First, the entry barriers protected the inefficient carriers, raising cost in the process. Second, the entry barriers excluded the potential efficient carriers. Third, regulation raised labour cost. The authors' policy recommendation was

98

clearly in favour of deregulation. A number of other studies showed that the average cost per passenger did not fall as the firm size increased (see for example, Eads, Nerlove, and Raduchel, 1969, Straszheim, 1969 and White, 1979). Thus, the airline industry was not a natural monopoly. Economies of vehicle size was a different matter altogether. Caves, Christensen and Tretheway (1984) find strong evidence that suggested that the larger the aircraft, other things, being equal, the lower was the unit cost especially for the long haul. Also, as Graham and Kaplan (1982) note, empirical evidence supported the existence of economies of density whereby unit cost fell when airlines added flights or added seats to existing flights.

In October 1974, the Civil Aeronautics Board (1974) prepared a study of the domestic route system of the 48 contiguous states. It found that the overall volume of service was excessive in relation to demand in competitive markets. Given the projection of relatively slow growth of demand, the study recommended that the award of new or additional route authority take place at a slower rate. Also in October 1974, the Ford administration established a National Commission on Regulatory Reform to study in depth the federal regulatory agencies. The aim was to eliminate regulations that increased costs the consumers. Senator Edward Kennedy was also convinced that government regulation did not serve the purpose in many cases. He joined hands with Harvard Professor Stephen Breyer to bring out the inefficiencies of existing regulation. Investigations were mainly concentrated on the regulation of air services of the CAB. The Kennedy hearings again brought out the inefficiencies that resulted from regulation, by comparing the experiences of the regulated airlines with the unregulated intrastate carriers. A CAB task force also prepared a report in July, 1975, which advocated deregulation. When Jimmy Carter became President, he endorsed the idea of deregulation. Meanwhile, Professor Alfred Kahn was appointed Chairman of the CAB in June 1977. Professor Kahn was a staunch supporter of airline deregulation. The trend towards liberalisation was set under the previous Chairman John Robson when the Board took a new position on the subject of discount fares (Bailey, Graham and Kaplan, 1985). Low fare applicants like World Airways were awarded new authority. 'Peanuts' fares proposed by Texas International and 'Supersaver' fares by American Airlines for off-peak flights were approved. Similarly, under Professor Kahn, Allegheny's 'Simple Saver' fares (offering discounts on multi-stop flights) and 'Tag-end' fares (offering discounts on flights with unusually low load factors) were approved.

Organised labour was uniformly opposed to deregulation. Before the Senate Commerce Committee, Subcommittee on Aviation, the labour unions jointly stated (Vietor, 1994, p. 53):

> We are vigorously opposed to legislation which our experience in this industry, our nation's history, human nature, and just plain common sense demonstrates to us will be anticonsumer, antiindustry, antilabor and therefore, antipublic interest.

The certificated carriers were, at first, opposed to deregulation or even to significant reforms. However, by mid 1977, a handful of airlines were in favour of deregulation. These airlines included United, Pacific Southwest, Air Wisconsin, Airwest and Continental. But other airlines were bitterly opposed to the idea. Consumer advocate Ralph Nader preferred regulatory reforms over deregulation. Nader was convinced that deregulation would jeopardise the interests of the consumers by forcing them to pay higher fares on less dense routes. He was also concerned about lower service quality and safety under the deregulatory environment.

In a move towards encouraging price competition, the CAB proposed, in April 1978, to allow fare reductions up to 50 percent without the Board's approval. Earlier, first class fares had to be 50 percent higher than coach fares. The proposal sought to do away with this requirement. At the same time, the CAB was liberalising entry and exit into the industry. As Meyer et al (1981, p. 51) observe:

> Multiple permissive entry policy awarded all applicants authority on the routes if they could demonstrate financial fitness.

By the middle of 1978 airline passenger miles were rising. The rate of return on equity was up to 16.3 percent and the load factor went up to 70 percent.

A bill was passed by the Senate in April, 1978, whereby airlines were given more freedom to compete and regulatory powers of the CAB were reduced. Similarly, in September 1978, the House passed a bill giving airlines more competitive freedom in setting fares and route structure. The stage was now set for the passage of the Airline Deregulation Act (ADA). On 24 October 1978, President Carter signed the Airline Deregulation Act into law. The Airline Deregulation Act relaxed gradually the CAB's regulation of the airline industry. The overriding theme of the ADA was competition - both actual and potential - to bring about the objectives of efficiency, innovation, low prices, and price/service options while at the same time encouraging efficient and well-managed carriers to earn adequate profits and to attract capital.

The main provisions of the Airline Deregulation Act were as follows. For the complete wording of the Airline Deregulation Act of 1978 and a description of the circumstances leading to the passage of the Act, see Miller (1981). First, the carriers were allowed to raise fares by five percent over and above adjusting fares upward by the rate of inflation. Second, the CAB was authorised to issue certificates for interstate and overseas transportation as long as the applicant was 'fit'. The burden of proof was now on the opponents that entry was inconsistent with public convenience and necessity. Third, the carriers were allowed to serve a new market every calendar year without CAB approval from 1979 to 1981. Fourth, the carriers were given authority to serve routes that were not being flown by the carriers that were certificated to fly them. Fifth, the carriers were required to give at least ninety days' notice to the CAB and the affected community before terminating or suspending service below an essential level. Sixth, the Act provided for a ten-year Essential Air Service (EAS) to small communities, which were likely to lose air service after the passage of the ADA. Payment of subsidy was also authorised to maintain essential air service.

The rate and route authority of the CAB was to phase out. Route authority of the Board was to end on 31 December 1983, while the Board's authority over domestic mergers, intercarrier agreements, and interlocking directorates was to be transferred to the Department of Justice on 1 January 1985. At that time, remaining tasks like international negotiations and small community air service were to be shifted to the Department of Transportation.

Conclusions

Economic regulation, in the true sense of the term, did not start until Civil Aeronautics Act of 1938 was passed. This Act remained the basis for regulation until the passage of the Airline Deregulation Act. The main theme of this chapter has been that economic regulation of airlines in the US was justified on the ground that it would promote public interest by enabling people to enjoy a safe and adequate transportation service provided by financially sound and reliable carriers. However, some studies found that regulation, in practice, did not promote public interest. One of the hypotheses that Jordan (1970) tested was that regulation protected the producers by helping them to form a cartel to obtain monopoly profit. The cartelisation hypothesis was supported by his analysis. During the regulation era, entry was effectively limited. Exits were controlled, and market shares of exiting carriers were transferred to one or more carriers. Price level was higher than it would have been under a deregulated environment. The hypothesis was also supported by the fact that lower quantity of service was produced than would have otherwise occurred and service quality was higher. Thus, the study found evidence of 'capture' of the benefits by the airlines. However, Jordan (1970) found the cartel to be imperfect.

According to Breyer and Stein (1982), three features of the airline industry make regulation inappropriate. First, individual markets and the industry as a whole can support many airlines of efficient size. Second, demand for air travel is highly cyclical. Load factors go down and costs per passenger go up during recessions. Industry profits will suffer if airlines are not allowed to reduce prices to attract more customers during recessions. Third, the cost of serving markets does not depend only on distance but also on air and ground congestion, season, time of day, availability of fuel and a whole host of other factors. Costs will also vary among carriers according to management style and employee relations.

Chapter 7

The Theory of Contestable Markets and US Airline Deregulation: A Survey

Introduction

Economists' ideal market structure from the point of view of efficient resource allocation has been 'perfect competition', characterised by a large number of buyers and sellers, homogeneous products, free entry and exit, and perfect knowledge on the part of buyers and sellers about the conditions in the market. Conditions of Pareto optimality are fulfilled by perfect competition. Although theoretically ideal, most markets, in reality, do not come close to the perfectly competitive ones. The markets for industrial goods, in particular, tend to be far removed from the perfectly competitive ideal. Yet the concept is very important to economists.

The quest for a type of market that will yield the same type of results as does perfect competition has led to the development of the theory of contestable markets. The concept was developed by Baumol, Panzar, Willig and others during the late 1970s and early 1980s. A contestable market may be defined as a market into which entry is absolutely free and exit is absolutely costless. A firm can enter such markets, earn a profit and then exit without incurring any costs other than those directly associated with production. Three characteristics of such markets are noteworthy. First, Baumol, Panzar and Willig (1982) have shown that in equilibrium, profit in such markets would be reduced to zero. Any positive profit would induce entry and result in undercutting incumbents' prices by entrants. Such a process will continue until all profits are reduced to zero. Second, such markets are characterised by lowest costs of production. Third, in a contestable market with two or more sellers, price in equilibrium will be equal to marginal cost.

Next, we review the major studies regarding the applicability of the theory of contestable markets to the airline industry. This is not a comprehensive survey. The studies are reviewed in chronological order.

Bailey and Panzar (1981)

The paper by Bailey and Panzar (1981) was probably the first paper, which attempted to apply the theory of contestable markets to the airline industry. They contend that contestable markets are compatible with the existence of economies of scale because such markets, even if served by just one firm, may have many characteristics of competitive markets, which are considered desirable. The paper argues that the theory is relevant to city-pair markets in the medium and long-haul routes served by local carriers during the two years following deregulation. They find them to be contestable. The authors base their conclusion on an examination of the pricing behaviour of local carriers, which faced the threat of potential competition from trunk carriers. The authors attempt to reconcile the fact that there are natural monopolies in many city-pair markets with the view that there is no need to regulate these markets. They argue that, although, it is true that there are no significant economies of scale in air transportation with regard to the entire system, city-pair markets enjoy economies of scale, for example, with respect to aircraft size. Economies of scale explain the existence of more monopoly city-pair markets than competitive markets in the US. See table 7.1.

Table 7.1 Nonstop Markets in the Domestic US for Trunk and Local Service Carriers (1 January 1980)

Distance	Number of Monopoly Markets	Number of Competitive Markets
0-200 miles	425	111
201-400 miles	294	106
406-600 miles	140	78
601 miles plus	320	230

Source: Bailey and Panzar (1981)

However, Bailey and Panzar state that economies of scale in city-pair markets do not result in entry barriers even if these markets are virtual monopolies because sunk costs are low. The lack of barriers to entry makes most city-pair markets readily contestable. The authors support their contention of minimal barriers to entry by noting that between 1 July 1978, and 1 July 1979, the 449 new non-stop services were introduced and 332 non-stop services were deleted. In more than half of the additions, the carriers had previously provided services from both airports.

The number of flights between any two cities is determined by economies of scale in aircraft size, the density of market demand and the desire to fly at particular times of day. The major portion of sunk costs in aviation is runways, towers and ground facilities. Ground facilities are generally, but not always, paid for by municipalities. Passenger terminals at major airports are paid for by airlines.

Bailey and Panzar (Bailey and Panzar, 1981, p. 134) point out:

> Explicit price competition was not encouraged until 1977 when downward flexibility was granted.

With the introduction of this flexibility, the divergence between standard coach fare (Standard Industry Fare Level or SIFL) and average fare increased with the average fares being lower than standard coach fares. However, for the third quarter of the 1979, prices were found to be higher in markets where only one carrier was permitted to serve compared with markets in which more than one carrier was authorised to serve. This goes against the contestability hypothesis. But this happened when the entry controls were not relaxed completely. Hence, some residual effects of regulation could have influenced the markets.

Bailey and Panzar's examination of commuter airline prices show that although these airlines had no constraints on prices, they did not charge any higher prices than the local service carriers. This pricing behaviour suggests that they faced potential competition from trunk carriers for city-pairs with a distance of less than 400 miles, whereas *potential* competition from trunk carriers for city-pairs with a distance of more than 400 miles was a check on prices for local service carriers. In the authors' view, local service monopolists were pricing competitively on longer routes after deregulation.

Graham, Kaplan and Sibley (1983)

Graham, Kaplan and Sibley (1983) try to test two hypotheses. First, many economists thought that regulation by the CAB was conducive to service competition which resulted in excess capacity. Thus, under regulation, fares determined by market forces should yield better capacity utilisation. Second, potential competition in the deregulated environment was supposed to keep fares at the competitive levels even in highly concentrated markets because of the high mobility of capital in the airline industry.

The authors emphasise that deregulation did not come in just one step. Steps towards deregulation was taken even before the passage of the Airline Deregulation Act (ADA) of 1978. An important step was taken in Spring of 1977 when 'Super Saver' fares approved. With the passage of the ADA in October, 1978, carriers were allowed to set fares as much as 10 percent above or 50 percent below a CAB standard fare. In May 1980, carriers were given unlimited flexibility regarding fares, thus virtually ending any governmental control over prices.

The CAB restricted routes in two ways. First, it restricted entry into the industry. Secondly, it limited the number of carriers allowed to compete in a given city-pair market. Normally, only major trunk carriers were allowed to serve long-haul markets while local-service carriers were limited to serving short-haul markets. These types of restrictions led passengers to use more interline connections although consumers prefer single line connections. Because these route restrictions were virtually abolished in December 1978, there were many route restructuring. Large and medium hubs received more flights than previously. Although the total number of flights to/from small communities (small hubs and nonhubs) declined, such communities now had more flights to large and medium hubs. The concentration of markets, as measured by the Herfindahl index, fell in general. The Herfindahl index is the sum of the squared market shares of all firms.

Fares established by the CAB were based only on distance. But distance was not the only factor affecting the cost of service. Other factors such as the volume of traffic, also affect cost. Moreover, the Board introduced another anomaly by setting rates below cost in short-haul markets and above cost in long-haul markets. The authors compared the distance-based formula fares (adjusted for inflation) with actual fares in 1980. As expected, actual fares as a percentage of DPFI (Domestic Passenger Fare Investigation) fares declined with a rise in length of haul and market density.

Costs are reduced if larger aircraft are used and load factors are higher. However, demand for convenient service may require more frequent flights using smaller aircraft at lower load factors. Tourist markets are expected to have larger aircraft and higher load factors because the sensitivity of tourists to service quality is less than that of business travellers. Longer haul markets are also expected to use larger aircraft and have higher load factors.

The hypothesis of excess capacity posits that regulation, by suppressing price competition and encouraging service competition, leads to more flights than what is justified by efficiency. Excess capacity would differ among markets because the structure of regulated fares did not match the structure of costs. One would expect that with increased price competition and less service competition, there would be less of a relationship between market structure and load factor.

The authors test the excess capacity hypothesis by comparing the relationship among load factors, distance, concentration and traffic volume for 1980 and 1976 with the relationship reported by Douglas and Miller (1974) for 1969. They use a methodology similar to that of Douglas and Miller except that they measure concentration by the Herfindahl index of the carriers' shares of the departures, and not by the number of carriers. Thus, average load factors are expressed as a loglinear function of distance, passenger per day and the Herfindahl index. Both OLS and 2SLS estimates show for 1976 and 1980 that load factors increased with increases in distance, density and concentration. However, Douglas and Miller find for 1969, that, while average load factors rose with passengers per day and concentration (i.e., with the number of carriers) for 1969, distance varied inversely with average load factors. The downward-sloping load-factor curve for 1969 is interpreted by Douglas and Miller as evidence that airlines were supplying excess capacity in potentially profitable long-haul markets. The estimated equations are in table 7.2.

Not only did load factors increase with distance for 1976 and 1980, but also load factors were higher for each distance in both of these years than in 1969. The authors concluded that the CAB had imposed wrong structure of fares in the late 1960s. The results for 1976 (when DPFI was introduced) show that DPFI helped to mitigate the excess service competition caused by the mismatch between fares and costs in long-haul markets. Although load factors and density are positively related for all three years, the higher coefficient of density (passengers per day) for 1980 was indicative of a greater increase in load factors in denser markets. The authors interpret the market concentration coefficient for 1980 as a decline in service competition resulting from increased price competition after deregulation.

Table 7.2 Equations Explaining Average Load Factors

	Constant	Ln Distance	Ln Pass. Per day	Ln Herfindahl	R^2
1. 1980-81	0.130	0.026	0.053	0.061	.33
OLS	(3.87)	(5.09)	(8.14)	(4.37)	
2. 1980-81	0.056	0.018	0.068	0.103	
2SLS	(1.21)	(2.81)	(6.25)	(4.66)	
3. 1976	0.123	0.029	0.047	0.127	.29
OLS	(3.21)	(5.88)	(7.83)	(8.20)	
4. 1976	0.042	0.025	0.067		
2SLS	(0.77)	(4.53)			

Source: Graham, Kaplan and Sibley (1983)

The authors do not think that service convenience declined as increasing load factors might suggest. Peak-load pricing increased, thus increasing the accessibility of time-sensitive passengers to peak flights.

To test the hypothesis of potential competition, they ask the question: do the firms in highly concentrated markets set fares higher than those in less concentrated but otherwise similar markets?

Cost of service is made a function of distance, traffic volume, level of convenience demanded, whether the markets involved one of the slot-constrained airports (i.e., the airports in New York, Chicago and/or Washington D.C.) and whether the market was served by newly-certified carriers (costs would be lower for newly-certified carriers). Thus, long run marginal cost of service is made a function of distance, number of passengers, load factor, presence of newly certified carriers and New York, Chicago and Washington D.C. dummies. Service quality is a function of tourist dummies (1 for tourist markets, namely, Florida, Hawaii, Las Vegas and Reno, and zero otherwise), product of per capita income in two cities, and other exogenous variables. Carriers can mark up fares above long-run marginal cost if demand elasticities are lower. Price elasticities in tourist markets are expected to be higher because of alternatives available such as changes in destinations and using other modes of transportation. The equilibrium market price is given by P = LRMC x markup where LRMC stands for long-run marginal cost. Markup depends upon barriers to entry, concentration, competitiveness of ground transportation and whether a market is a tourist market. Price is thus made a function of distance, number of passengers, whether the markets involved service to New York, Chicago or Washington DC, tourist dummies, income and whether the markets involved services by newly certified carriers. Price is measured by average yield (coach fare per revenue passenger mile). The model is estimated using both OLS and 2SLS. The estimates are quite similar.

The results are mostly as expected. Average fare per mile declined as distance rose to 1,000 miles, remained the same for distance between 1,000 miles and 2,000 miles and declined again for distance above 2,000 miles. Density did not have much effect on fares (the coefficient was insignificant). Fares were related to passengers' value of time – the coefficient on tourist markets was negative (tourist markets were estimated to have ten percent lower fares). The income coefficient was positive. Fares were higher in markets serving slot-constrained airports, i.e., airports in New York, Chicago and Washington DC. The markets served by newly certified carriers had lower fares. Finally, one of the most important results was that the market concentration had a positive impact on fares in the relatively unconcentrated markets.

Graham, Kaplan and Sibley conclude that in many ways, the airline market was behaving in ways the economists predicted it would. There was a rise in the load factor. Distance, demand for convenient service and competition from newly certified carriers had substantial impacts on fares. However, the positive relationship of fares to market concentration goes against the contestability hypothesis. Such an occurrence can be interpreted as indicating that potential competition was not working as hypothesised by the contestability theory. Two arguments are normally proposed in favour of contestability in airline markets: absence of sunk costs, and expectation by prospective entrants that incumbents' prices will not change in response to entry. But these assumptions may not hold. Moreover, as Graham, Kaplan and Sibley (p. 137) note, "The literature does not provide an explicit way of proving contestability".

Bailey, Graham and Kaplan (1985)

Bailey, Graham and Kaplan (BGK hereinafter) (1985) argue that airline markets are not perfectly contestable. The result is that prices in monopolistic markets tend to be higher than in markets, which are more competitive in nature.

The theory of contestable markets, which provides the theoretical basis for deregulation of airlines, is based on the following assumptions (Bailey, Graham and Kaplan, 1985, pp. 154-55):

(1) all factors of production are mobile among markets, (2) consumers are willing and able to switch quickly among suppliers, and (3) existing firms are unable to change their prices quickly in response to the entry of a new firm.

Obviously, it is unlikely that airline industry would satisfy all the assumptions above.

BGK believe that the contestability of airline markets is supported by the high degree of mobility of aircraft and by the fact that ground facilities needed to operate airlines in a city-pair market can easily be leased. However, the authors note that the hypothesis of contestability is somewhat undermined by the presence of some sunk costs. Again, entrants may not readily become effective competitors because it takes some time to for them to establish a favourable reputation. Advertising cost is, in this sense, a sunk cost. The authors also question the traditional belief of rigidity of incumbents' prices (as the contestability theory implies) because often, particularly in the early 1980s, incumbents matched the entrants' prices without any delay.

However, there is a behavioural aspect to the contestability hypothesis. Behavioural contestability would be found if fares are independent of market structure and depend only on costs of serving a particular city-pair market. The important question in this respect is whether the market structure is endogenous, i.e., determined by other factors. Volume of traffic and structure of market are jointly determined because market structure would be determined by technology and demand. As Bailey, Graham and Kaplan (1985, p. 155) observe:

However, structure may not be uniquely determined by technology and traffic volume. If average costs are flat over a wide range of outputs, there may be a wide range of possible industry structures. The observed structure may thus reflect a history of random shocks that determine the relative sizes of the existing firms. In this case industry structure can only be bounded by economic analysis and the observed structure is a function of unobserved variables.

This sort of indeterminacy of market structure is further complicated because the impact of previous regulation was still affecting airline markets.

BGK test the contestability hypothesis in two ways. In one model, they assume market structure to be exogenously determined. Concentrated markets have higher fares under this model. In the second model, fares are endogenous and thus are independent of the levels of concentration. BGK's econometric testing finds that the market structure should be considered exogenous. This is consistent with the earlier study by Graham, Kaplan and Sibley.

To test the contestability hypothesis, BGK estimate a system of simultaneous equations. Their model here is very similar to that of Graham, Kaplan and Sibley. The cost function makes average cost of serving a passenger in a given market a function of distance, density (the number of passengers carried), whether it involves service to a slot-constrained airports (namely, airports in New York, Chicago and Washington DC), whether it is served by newly certified carrier (which had lower costs) and time sensitivity of passengers. Price is assumed to be given by markup (a function of market structure) multiplied by average cost. The demand function makes density a function of price, distance, income of the travellers and time sensitivity of travellers. When structure is treated as an endogenous variable, structure is made a function of density, distance and hub. Price is measured by average yield. Personal income (the product of per capita income of two cities) is used as a proxy for time sensitivity. Hub and slot restricted variables take the form of dummies. Structure is measured by Herfindahl index and the population of the two cities served by each market.

BGK find that tourist markets had lower fares than the non-tourist markets. Fares were also higher in markets where incomes were higher. Thus, fares varied with time sensitivity of passengers. Average fares were found to be lower for markets in which newly certified carriers served. The results of the study indicate that established carriers did not reduce fares fearing potential entry. Only when entry had occurred did these airlines match the newcomer's price. Bailey, Graham and Kaplan, p. 164) remark:

> It should be emphasised that this finding does not rule out the possibility that contestability among the rival established airlines is working to keep fares equal to the levels of their costs.

The fare in a market with two equal-sized competitors was found to be six percent lower than monopoly levels whereas a market with four equal-sized competitors was found to have a fare, which was 11 percent below the monopoly level.

Overall, their study does not fully support the contestability hypothesis, at least during the first few years after deregulation. Carriers operating in concentrated markets possessed sufficient powers to set fares above costs. But the degree of this power was not very high.

Moore (1986)

The relationship of fares to a measure of market contestability is crucial as a test of contestability. Moore (1986) regresses coach fares in 1983 and in 1976 on the length of flight, dummy variables for various market structures, population of the city of origin and dummy variables for the major cities of destinations. The results show that fares were lower for markets with five or more carriers. Compared with 1976, in 1983 coach fares rose by 40 percent in real terms for markets served by only one or two carriers, whereas markets served by five or more carriers experienced a rise of only three percent in coach fares in real terms during the same period.

Moore employs another test for contestability. He regresses the ratio of 1983 fares to 1976 fares on air miles and the change in the number of carriers from 1976 to 1983. The regressions were run for the whole sample, for the long haul markets and for all markets except the long haul markets. For the whole sample and for the sample of all markets except the long haul, the change in the number of carriers had a significant effect on the ratio of fares. Addition of one carrier would reduce the fares in 1983 by 15 percent relative to fares in 1976 in all except the long-haul markets. These results go against the applicability of contestability theory to airline markets.

Morrison and Winston (1986)

Morrison and Winston (1986) distinguish between perfect contestability as developed by Baumol, Panzar and Willig (1982), and imperfect contestability as developed by Bain (1949, 1951). Bain recognised long ago that potential competition would influence the conduct and performance of sellers in a market. Baumol, Panzar and Willig go a step further. They show that when entry and exit are costless, potential competition can generate welfare maximising performance.

Morrison and Winston develop tests for both perfect contestability and imperfect contestability. Their study uses more recent data, 1983, than many of the previous studies. It also differs from other studies in that it uses a more direct measure of consumer welfare, i.e., compensating variation. The basis of their analysis is a multinomial logit model of inter-city passenger demand for business and pleasure travellers. In that model, the probability of choosing a particular mode of transportation (i.e., auto, bus, rail) is a function of the fare, trip time and time between departures of all modes. Using a procedure developed by Harvey and Rosen, Morrison and Winston calculate compensating variation measuring the difference between the welfare of passengers in the deregulated environment prevailing during 1983 and the optimal level of welfare.

A potential carrier on a route is defined here as a carrier that served one of the two airports but did not serve the route. Perfect contestability implies that the measure of welfare change would be equal to zero for markets having at least one potential competitor. For none of the 769 markets considered by Morrison and Winston did the welfare change measures equal zero. Deregulated welfare and socially optimum welfare differed by approximately 2.5 billion dollars. Thus, airline markets were found not to be perfectly contestable.

Imperfect contestability would imply that for a given route, the welfare change measure is influenced by the number of actual and potential carriers on the route. In such a market, the gap between optimal and actual welfare is reduced by an increase in the number of actual and potential carriers. The regression results indicate that every additional potential competitor reduced the difference between optimal and actual welfare per traveller by .44 cents per mile, while each potential competitor reduced the difference per traveller by .15 cents per mile. Therefore, one actual competitor would have the same influence on welfare as three potential competitors. Thus, the study finds that imperfect contestability held in the airline markets.

Sinha (1987)

While other studies concentrate on major routes in the United States, Sinha studies the applicability of the theory to city-pair markets involving a small hub, Omaha, Nebraska. He follows Moore's methodology. Table 7.3 gives the number of carriers serving markets in 1983, sample size and mean of the ratio of 1983 to 1976 deflated fares for 28 markets involving Omaha.

Table 7.3   Ratio of 1983 to 1976 Deflated Coach Fares by the Number of Carriers in 1983 for Omaha

Number of carriers in 1983	Sample size	Mean of ratio of fares
1	8	1.5617
2	6	1.5969
3	7	1.3762
4	5	1.2334
5	1	1.2531
6	1	1.3842

Source: Sinha (1987)

The results show that as the number of carriers went up from 1 to 4, the increase in fares in real terms dropped from 56 percent to 23 percent when 1976 fares are compared with 1983 fares. Then, as the number of carriers rose further, there was some rise in fares but the sample size was too small to put any credence in such results. Thus, the actual number of carriers serving the market seemed to have an effect on fares.

To carry the analysis further, the ratio of deflated fares is regressed on distance (air miles) and the change in the number of carriers. The results using OLS are as follows:

$$FARE = 1.6699 - 0.123 \text{ CHACAR} - 0.0002 \text{ DIST} \qquad R^2 = 0.19 \qquad (8.1)$$
$$(19.804) \quad (-2.783) \qquad (-2.225)$$

where CHACAR stands for change in the number of carriers and DIST stands for distance. The results show that an increase in the number of carriers by one will reduced fare by 12.3 percent. This seems to go against the perfect contestability hypothesis.

Hurdle et al (1989)

The term 'imperfect contestability' is used to mean different things. Whereas Morrison and Winston (1986) use imperfect contestability to mean 'not perfectly contestable', Hurdle et al use the same term to mean 'almost perfectly contestable'. To test the contestability hypothesis, they use a variable, which they call the Likely Potential Entrants (or LPEs). There are three possibilities here – LPEs may have no effect, a significant but less than the effects of those who are already serving the market or LPEs can have the same effect as the incumbents. In this last case, LPEs are actual competitors other than the incumbents and are called OCs (Other Competitors).

The study uses the city pair markets rather than carriers as the unit of observation. Even though Morrison and Winston consider the threat of entry, this study treats the issue more extensively. All data pertain to 1985. The total number of city pair markets used in the study is 867. Yield is used as the measure of market performance. Yield is the average revenue (for a city pair market) per passenger mile. Such calculations do not include connecting passengers but include only non-stop and direct passengers (who do not change planes even though they stop at a airport). An incumbent for a city pair is defined as one having the following characteristics: (1) offered non-stop service (2) made at least one hundred flights on the city pair during 1985 (3) was not a commuter carrier (where a commuter carrier is defined as one having less than 60 seats – commuter carriers are not included because data on commuter carriers are incomplete and the commuter carriers have less effect on competition because of the perception of the passengers that commuter carriers offer lower levels of comfort and are less safe).

If the city pair market is not sufficiently large enough to support at least two carriers, it is designated as a natural monopoly. 11.2 percent of the city pair markets are designated as natural monopolies because the passengers on these markets fall below the minimum efficient scale (MES). The MES is defined as one flight per day with 72.4035 passengers. There are no LPEs/OCs on these city pair markets. City pair markets, which are not designated as natural monopolies are divided into two groups. Proportion Beyond (PB) is defined as those passengers whose origin or destination was other than the end points of the city pair. PB of 0.4694 is used as the base point. Any city pair market with a PB of less than the base point is considered a route for which feed does not pose a significant entry deterrent. For these city pair markets, LPEs/OCCs are any carrier that served at least one city pair market but not on the particular city pair market. For the other city pair markets, LPEs/OCs are determined on the basis of combined enplanements at the two endpoints. Non-incumbent carriers with combined enplanements at the two end points at least of the half of the average of the incumbents are considered LPEs/OCs.

They estimate four different regressions to explain yield using a variety of independent variables. Since LPEs/OCs are defined above, the other variables are explained as follows:

Herfindahl (H) = Herfindahl measure of concentration of the incumbents

Adjusted Herfindahl (AH) = $1/[1/H) + OC]$.

DIST = Great circle distance between two airports (natural log is taken because it is expected that yield will have a non-linear relationship with distance).

Average Plane Size (APS) = This is calculated by dividing the number of available seats on the city pair market divided by the number of departures.

Density = Total number of revenue passengers flying non-stop on the city pair (including those travelling beyond one or both end points). It is a measure of economies of scale and scope realised in such things as advertising and utilisation of airport facilities. Natural log of density is used because it is surmised that these economies fall as distance increases.

Load Factor = The number of revenue passengers on the city pair divided by the number of available seats.

Slot Dummy = Dummy variable indicating slot constraints (Kennedy and LaGuardia in New York, O'Hare in Chicago and National in Washington) at one end point.

Commuter Dummy = Dummy variable indicating at least one commuter.

Proportional Single Plane = Proportion of passengers travelling on the city pair using one plane.

The four regressions estimated are of the following forms:

Yield = f (Herfindahl, Herfindahl Interactions, Cost Variables)   (8.2)

Yield = f (Herfindahl, Likely Potential Entrants, Herfindahl Interactions, Cost Variables)   (8.3)

Yield = f (Adjusted Herfindahl, Adjusted Herfindahl Interactions, Cost Variables)   (8.4)

Yield = f (Cost Variables)   (8.5)

Table 7.4 Regression Coefficients Explaining 1985 Yields on Non-stop City Pairs

Variables	Regression 1	Regression 2	Regression 3	Regression 4
Constant	0.8657 (0.055)	0.9023 (0.051)	0.9778 (0.040)	0.9662 (0.051)
Herfindahl	0.0195 (0.023)	-0.0144 (0.022)		0.1267 (0.029)
Adjusted Herfindahl			-0.0898 (0.019)	-0.2065 (0.029)
Likely Potential Entrants		-0.0016 (0.0001)		-0.0018 (0.0003)
Proportional Single Plane x Herfindahl	0.0682 (0.024)	0.0773 (0.022)		-0.1019 (0.033)
Slot Dummy x Herfindahl	-0.0105 (0.009)	0.0068 (0.008)		0.0061 (0.011)
Commuter Dummy x Herfindahl	0.0498 (0.010)	0.0602 (0.009)		0.0474 (0.013)
Proportional Single Plane x Adjusted Herfindahl			0.1881 (0.023)	0.2457 (0.037)
Slot Dummy x Adjusted Herfindahl			0.0183 (0.013)	0.0045 (0.018)
Commuter Dummy x Adjusted Herfindahl			0.0816 (0.013)	0.0304 (0.019)
Log of Distance	-0.1079 (0.005)	-0.1050 (0.005)	-0.1064 (0.005)	-0.1096 (0.005)
Average Plane Size	0.00005 (0.00009)	0.00012 (0.00008)	0.00014 (0.00008)	0.00015 (0.00008)
Load Factor	-0.2052 (0.033)	-0.1850 (0.031)	-0.1724 (0.029)	-0.1853 (0.030)
Log of Density	0.0079 (0.004)	0.0048 (0.004)	-0.0024 (0.003)	0.0023 (0.004)
R^2	0.69	0.74	0.74	0.76

Note: Standard errors are in parentheses

Source: Hurdle, Johnson, Joskow, Werden and Williams (1989)

The first three regressions are used to test whether the included structural variables affect yields. The fourth regression tests perfect contestability. The results are given in the table 7.4. The regressions showthat both distance and load factors are significantly negatively correlated with yield. These are as expected. The coefficients on average plane size and density are not significant. But, they do not have the expected signs in most cases. The coefficient on the interactions of proportional single plane with Herfindahl and adjusted Herfindahl are positive and significant which means that connecting service affected fares for non-stop service. On the other hand, the coefficients on the interaction of slot with Herfindahl and adjusted Herfindahl are both insignificant implying that slot constraints were not important determinants of fares. The authors attribute this result to the fact that the cities, which had a slot constrained airport also had an airport which is not slot constrained. The coefficients on the interaction of commuter with Herfindahl and adjusted Herfindahl are significant and positive suggesting that commuter airlines did not have the effect of reducing fares. This is in contrast to what we expect.

The individual coefficients on the Herfindahl index and the adjusted Herfindahl index are not very useful because these cannot be used directly for hypothesis testing. For example, in regression 1, the partial derivative of yield with respect to the Herfindahl index gives us the linear combination of proportional single plane, slot constraint and commuter dummy equal to zero. But all these three variables can take on many values and thus, various combinations of these values are relevant here.

The authors do further testing (not shown here). They test the hypothesis that all market structure coefficients are jointly zero. For each regression, they reject the hypothesis. Thus, they conclude that the market structure mattered quite a lot. For example, they find that in the absence of any potential entrants or other competitors, a merger of the two incumbents had the effect of increasing the yield by 2.5 to 8.2 cents. There is a drawback to using hypothesis testing using regressions in that it involves the imposition of prior beliefs about the functional form and the choice and measurements of explanatory variables. Thus, the authors follow up the results of regressions using nonparametric regression trees. While the nonparametric regression trees do not eliminate the need for prior beliefs, they certainly reduce the need for prior beliefs to a great extent. Again, the authors get the same result that market structure mattered. The nonparametric regression trees showed that the following variables measuring market structure mattered – the number and size distribution incumbents and the number of potential entrants. Only in those cases where the economies of scale or economies did not pose a significant entry deterrent, the degree of incumbent concentration did not matter. In all other cases, the degree of incumbent concentration highly mattered.

Conclusions

A perusal of the literature on contestability and airline markets reveals diverse opinions among economists on the subject. In general, the early studies, carried out mostly by the proponents of the theory of contestable markets seem to be more optimistic about the applicability of the theory to the airline industry. The study by Panzar and Bailey (1981) is a case in point. However, doubts about the applicability probably were cast first by Graham, Kaplan and Sibley (1983). Later writers have been less enthusiastic about the applicability.

Morrison and Winston (1986) add a new dimension to the controversy as they distinguish between perfect contestability and imperfect contestability. They find that imperfect contestability holds in the airline industry. This distinction has important policy implications. The existence of imperfect contestability means that both actual and potential competition need to be encouraged. Hurdle et al (1989) give another twist to the issue of imperfect contestability. Whereas in Morrison and Winston imperfect contestability means 'not perfectly contestable', in Hurdle et al, it means 'almost perfectly contestable'.

Some authors argue that contestability may hold sway in the airlines markets in the long run but not in the short run. About the early studies, some commentators have raised the question whether sufficient time had passed since airline deregulation to test for contestability.

Studies following that of Bailey and Panzar (1981), have almost consistently shown that actual competition rather than potential competition plays a more significant role. Obviously, not all the requirements for contestability are fulfilled by the airline industry. First, all the airlines do not have the same cost structures, as the contestability theory requires. Second, sunk costs at airports impede contestability. Slot or noise constraints restrict entry. The latter studies have led Baumol and Willig to change their stand on the issue somewhat. Thus, Baumol and Willig (1986, p. 15) observe:

In the initial enthusiasm with which we described contestability, we agreed with this assessment, and more than once cited the airline industry as a case in point, using the metaphoric argument that investment in aircraft do not incur any sunk cost because they constitute "capital on wings". Reconsideration has led us to adopt a more qualified position on this score. We now believe that transportation by trucks, barges, and even buses may be more highly contestable than passenger air transportation.

On the issue of perfect contestability, Baumol (1982, p. 4) observes:

> Perfect contestability serves not primarily as a description of reality, but as a benchmark for desirable industrial organization which was available to us before.

Although we find widely differing views among the economists on the subject, the theory of contestability has provided for an alternative criterion for judging market performance in many industries including the airline industry. This is, by no means, an insignificant contribution.

What reduces the contestability of airlines? A number of factors make it difficult for a newcomer to compete effectively with the incumbents. These include apprehensions regarding safety of the new airlines, absence of a brand name, frequent flier programs of the established airlines, computer reservation systems which discriminate against the new entrants, high costs of access to airport terminals.

Chapter 8

Effects of Airline Deregulation in the US

Introduction

We looked at the evolution of regulation and deregulation of airlines in the US in the light of the theories of regulation in chapter 6. It is clear from the discussion in chapter 6 that economists played a major role in bringing out the inefficiencies of airline regulation. In this chapter, we turn to study the effects of airline deregulation in its various aspects. Sinha (1999) has a brief discussion of the effects.

It is important to define the various categories of airports in the US. The Federal Aviation Administration divides all airports in the US into the following categories: large hubs, medium hubs, small hubs and nonhubs. Communities that enplane one percent or more of the total passengers are called large hubs; communities enplaning between 0.25 and 0.99 percent are called medium hubs; communities that enplane between 0.05 and 0.24 are called small hubs; communities that enplane less than 0.05 percent are called nonhubs.

Effects on Airfares

Morrison and Winston (1997) estimate that airfares fell 33 percent in real terms between 1976 and 1993. While not all of the drop could be attributed to airline deregulation, Morrison and Winston estimate that at least 60 percent of the fall (which is a 20 percent fall in the fares) can be accounted for by airline deregulation.

While it is true that on an average basis, all air passengers have enjoyed lower airfares, passengers at large and medium airports have benefited more. Morrison and Winston attribute this to competition and cost – that is, there is lack of competition in the small hubs and nonhubs and the cost of serving passengers at these airports is higher.

Table 8.1   Number of and Traffic at FAA Large, Medium and Small Hubs, 1969-97

Year	Large hubs (number)	Large-hub traffic (%)	Medium Hubs (number)	Medium-hub traffic (%)	Small hubs (number)	Small hubs (%)
1969	22	69.7	38	20.4	86	9.9
1973	25	68.4	39	18.4	84	9.0
1977	25	68.1	39	18.4	92	10.2
1981	24	70.2	40	19.0	72	7.9
1985	26	72.8	37	18.1	61	6.7
1989	28	73.0	34	17.7	63	7.0
1993	25	72.6	30	16.9	68	8.0
1997	29	74.8	31	16.0	60	6.7

Source: Reynolds-Feighan (2000)

At present, the level of competition at large and medium hubs is almost equal whereas competition is much less at small hubs and nonhubs. As shown by Morrison and Winston (1997), even though the gap is narrowing, the number of effective competitors in medium hubs has been higher than in large hubs since the mid-1970s. To measure effective competition, the authors use the inverse of the Herfindahl index. As far as the costs are concerned, there are two sources of economies. Cost per seat mile will be lower for larger aircraft and higher load factor. Large and medium hubs are served by larger aircraft and they have higher load factor. On the other hand, routes where the number of passengers is rather low will be served by smaller aircraft but with a lower frequency of service than otherwise.

Morrison and Winston (1997) find that differences in aircraft size explains nearly 40 percent of the differences in fares. Differences in load factors explain about 50 percent of the differences in fares. The differences in competition explain only 10 percent of the differences. Morrison and Winston (1990) also find that increased competition has the effect of lowering fares. However, the effect is not as pronounced in the slot-controlled airports. They also find that an airline's entry and exit behaviour is influenced much more by its own network than its competitors' networks.

Morrison and Winston (1997) estimate that on an average, one-way fares for comparable distances elsewhere were higher by $17 to $22 (or by 11 to 15 percent) in 1996 for flights involving O'Hare, LaGuardia and National but not for Kennedy. They suggest congestion pricing as a way to increase competition. According to the current system, airport fees vary according to the weight of the aircraft. Charges for the larger aircraft are higher than those for the smaller aircraft (such as those used by commuter airlines). The congestion pricing is based on the idea that arrivals are departures should vary according to the time of the day. Thus, arrivals and departures at peak times will be charged higher fees because these impose costs (in the form of delays) on other arrivals and departures. On the other hand, fees for the off-peak times will be low.

The demand for air service is subject to cyclical fluctuations. Airfares also exhibit cyclical fluctuations. The post-deregulation period has been marked by substantial increases in airfares from time to time. Morrison and Winston (see for example, Morrison and Winston, 1995) have always maintained that airfares are lower than they would have been under regulation.

Effects on Air Service

Daily departures are one indication of service. Department of Transportation data indicate that daily departures have increased significantly at large and medium hubs, moderately at small hubs and marginally at nonhubs. However, daily departures as an indicator of service has the drawback that it does not take into account the changes in the number of connecting flights. The increased use of the hub and spoke operations during the post-deregulation era has meant that passengers flying from small and nonhubs have experienced an increase in the number of connecting flights. The total number of non-stop flights have also increased after deregulation.

One area in which regulation has remained is with regard to the slot-constrained airports. Four airports designated as slot-constrained are Kennedy and LaGuardia airports in New York, O'Hare in Chicago and National in Washington, DC. Limits on the number of arrivals and departures in the slot-constrained airports to reduce congestion have been enforced since the late 1960s. The regulation had the effect of reducing departures and therefore, competition.

Department of Transportation is taking measures to increase the slots at slot-constrained airports and to encourage the low-fare carriers to compete in the slot-constrained airports. However, research by Morrison and Winston (1997) indicate that the lack of competition from the low-cost airlines at the slot-constrained airports is not a serious problem. While the low-cost Southwest Airlines has the policy of avoiding the slot-constrained airports, other low-cost airlines do serve the slot-constrained airports as much as they serve the non-slot constrained airports. Thus, the more effective way of solving the problem is to introduce congestion pricing.

Effects of Hubs on Consumers and Airlines

The hub and spoke system did exist even before deregulation but the scale was quite limited. After deregulation, the airlines have been following the hub and spoke system to a much greater extent. Several times a day, the carriers schedule 'banks' of flights in and out of their hubs (Air Transport Association, 2000). Each 'bank' lasts for about 45 minutes during which many aeroplanes arrive one after another so that the passengers can conveniently catch their connecting flights. They are thus able to keep the passengers all the way through to their final destinations. Passengers are also spared the hassles of changing airlines (and thus, moving luggage). All major airlines in the United States have hubs – multiple hubs for a single airline also exists in some cases. A number of factors determine the location of the hub for an airline. Airlines are likely to have their hubs in cities where they have a significant number of origin and destination passengers.

Borenstein (1989), Berry (1990) and others discuss the advantages that hubs give to the airlines. First, airlines are able to serve many more markets than they would have been under point to point service. Second, Borenstein also finds that airlines can charge higher prices for flights involving their hub airports. However, this applies to flights from the hubs rather than to the hubs.

Third, the other airlines serving the same routes as the dominant carrier are unable to charge the higher fare that the dominant airline charges. The dominant airline has control over the market because it offers more frequent and convenient arrival and departure times from the hubs. Fourth, the larger the share the dominant airline has, more attractive it becomes to the passengers.

124

Fifth, the airlines may be able to offer more frequent flights than when non-stop flights are offered. Sixth, in many cases, an airline with a large presence at an airport may be able to exercise bureaucratic control because it is often an important source of finance at that airport. This may help the airline to block entry or to prevent the expansion of other airlines' operations. Sixth, the hub and spoke system also helps the airlines to increase their load factors.

Hubbing can increase the number of miles to be flown by those passengers who would otherwise fly directly to their destinations. Thus, hubbing can reduce total costs only if there are sufficient economies of scale in plane size. Only in such cases, the higher costs of flying passengers a greater number of miles can be overcome. Out of the eight major airlines, namely, American, United, Delta, Northwest, US Air, Continental, TWA and Southwest, all except Southwest follow the hub and spoke strategy.

Hubs are not an unmixed blessing for the airlines. The airlines need to maintain a large number of ground service staff to do a variety of tasks – these include helping passengers with their connecting flights and handling their luggage. Since there are only a handful of 'banks' each day, the additional ground staff that are needed during each bank remain mostly idle at other times, thus increasing unit costs (Air Transport Association, 2000).

Moreover, inclement weather at the hub can disrupt the operations of the whole system of the carrier. Also, in many airports, there is an acute problem of congestion during the bank periods. Thus, these costs have to be weighed by the carriers against the benefits. Even though a number of carriers scaled down their hub operations after 1993, the fact that the carriers are still maintaining their hubs is testimony that on the whole, the airlines find the system to be beneficial.

As pointed out earlier, increased use of the hub and spoke system has benefited passengers from small and nonhubs because they now have more connecting flights.

Effects on Concentration of Airlines

Borenstein (1992) shows that there has been an increase in the concentration in the airline industry in the US after deregulation. Caves, Christensen and Tretheway (1984) had shown that economies of density (the additional number of passengers on a given set of routes) and the length of individual flights were important determinants of costs of the airlines and therefore, of competition among the airlines.

Kim and Singal (1993) also find that the dominant carrier is able to charge a higher fare. The mergers and acquisitions have increased concentration in the industry. Six largest carriers had a 62 percent of all domestic traffic in 1985. The same went up to 86 percent in early 1990s. The hub and spoke system, travel agent commission over-rides, frequent flier programs and computer reservation systems also tend to increase concentration.

Leahy (1994) calculates the Herfindahl-Hirshman index for the top 150 markets during the period from 1979 to 1988. The Herfindahl-Hirshman index, which takes the market share of each firm, calculates its square, then adds up the total for all the firms in the sector. Leahy estimates the following regression:

$$\text{PCH} = 85.5 - 0.0002 \text{ PAX} - 0.021 \text{ DIST} - 0.015 \text{ H79} \qquad (8.1)$$
$$\phantom{\text{PCH} = 85.5}\ \ (2.78) \qquad\quad (4.52) \qquad\quad (8.02)$$
$$R^2 = 0.35 \quad F = 25.9$$

In equation (8.1), PCH is the percentage change in the Herfindahl-Hirshman index over the period from 1979-1988, PAX is the number of passengers in the Department of Transportation's Origin and Destination Survey in 1988, DIST is the distance between the two airports and H79 is the Herfindahl-Hirshman index for 1979. The significance of the coefficients at the 1 percent level implies that economies of density (measured by the number of passengers variable PAX), distance and the beginning value of the Herfindahl-Hirshman index are important determinants of the changes in concentration in the airline industry during the post-deregulation period.

Effects of Entry of Low Fare Airlines

Since the passage of the Airline Deregulation Act in 1978, a number of low fare airlines have entered the US airline markets. Some of these airlines, however, have not survived.

There have been many studies, which look at the effects of entry of low cost airlines. The earlier studies use data for the period immediately following airline deregulation. For example, Bailey, Graham and Kaplan

(1985) use data for 1980-81 and their regressions find that newly certificated carriers affected yields negatively and significantly. Strassman (1990) uses 1980 data to find similar results.

Windle and Dresner (1995) use more recent data. Domestic origin-destination quarterly data for 200 top US domestic city-pair markets for three years (1991-94) are used in this study. They estimate two equations explaining price (or fare). The equations are

$$PRICE = \beta_0 + \beta_1 HERF + \beta_2 DIST + \beta_3 DIST^2 + \beta_4 PASS + \beta_5 SLOT$$

$$+ \beta_6 VACATION + \beta_7 HAWAII + \sum_{t=8}^{18} \beta_t QUARTER_t \qquad (8.2)$$

$$PRICE = \alpha_0 + \alpha_1 HERF + \alpha_2 DIST + \alpha_3 DIST^2 + \alpha_4 PASS + \alpha_5 SLOT$$
$$+ \alpha_6 VACATION + \alpha_7 HAWAII$$

$$+ \sum_{t=8}^{18} \beta_t QUARTER_t + \sum_{j=19}^{46} \beta_j CARRIER_j \qquad (8.3)$$

where PRICE is average one-way fare for all carriers on a route between two cities, HERF is Herfindahl index for a route, DIST is the great circle, $DIST^2$ is the DIST squared, PASS is total revenue passengers on the route, and SLOT is a dummy taking a value of 1 if one or both cities has slot-controlled airports and 0 otherwise. VACATION is a dummy taking a value of 1 if one of the two cities is in Florida, Nevada, Hawaii, or Puerto Rico and 0 otherwise. HAWAII is a dummy taking a value of 1 if the route is intra-Hawaiian and 0 otherwise. $QUARTER_t$s are dummy variables for each quarter of the sample (except the base quarter) to account for changes in prices over time. $CARRIER_j$s are dummy variables to account for different pricing strategies of the carriers. In effect, these are a number of dummies to account for the presence of 29 carriers, which include many large (like United) and many small (like Valuejet) airlines.

Thus, the independent variables include a number of demand, cost and market structure variables. The two equations are estimated by using the instrumental variable method because of the endogeneity of HERF and PASS. The coefficients on HERF and PASS are positive and significant for equation (8.2) and but not for equation (8.3). Thus, the estimated coefficient on HERF from equation (8.2) says that higher concentration leads to a higher price when individual carrier effects are not considered. The results from equation (8.3) show that individual firm effects outweighed the effects of concentration. The presence of a certain airline was more important than the low HERF in reducing price. PASS has both demand and cost side characteristics. Thus, it is a more complicated variable. From the cost side, an increase in the number of passengers can reduce price because it leads to cost economies. From the demand side, an increase in traffic can lead to an increase in price.

The most important result from the estimated equation (8.3) is that the presence of low fare airlines such as Southwest and Valuejet had the effect of lowering price significantly.

Vowles (2000) uses cross section data to fit a regression of the following form to determine the effects of low fare air carriers on airfares:

$$\text{FARE} = \beta_0 + \beta_1 \text{ DISTANCE} + \beta_2 \text{ RESORT} + \beta_3 \text{ WNFACTOR} + \beta_4 \text{HUB} + \beta_5 \text{LOW} + \beta_6 \text{LOWCARMS} + \beta_7 \text{LCMS} + \varepsilon \qquad (8.4)$$

where FARE is the average fare. The average fare data are taken from the US Department of Transportation's *Domestic Airline Fares Consumer Report* for the first quarter of 1997. The fare is calculated by dividing the aggregate fares paid by all passengers by the number of total revenue passengers. DISTANCE comes from the same source and measures the non-stop distance between two cities. RESORT is a dummy variable taking a value of one in case the destination is a resort destination and zero otherwise. WNFACTOR is another dummy which takes the value of one if one of the cities involved is in the Southwest and zero otherwise. HUB is also a dummy taking a value of one if one or both cities are designated as hubs and zero otherwise. In total, 19 cities are designated as hubs. LOW is again a dummy variable showing the presence of a low fare carrier. LOWCARMS is the market share of the lowest fare carrier. Finally, LCMS is the market share of the largest carrier.

The regression results show that the coefficients on DIST, HUB and LCMS have positive signs whereas the coefficients on RESORT, WNFACTOR, LOW and LOWCARMS have negative signs. All coefficients are found to be significant at the 1 percent level. The coefficient on LOW is found to indicate that the presence of a low fare carrier reduced fares by \$45.75.

Effects on Small Communities

The literature since the passage of the Airline Deregulation Act in 1978 has devoted much less attention to the small communities. Most empirical studies have focussed on airline markets involving hubs. The involvement of the government in the provision of air service in the small communities has been long.

Before deregulation, services to about 150 communities by local service carriers were being subsidised. These local service carriers had earlier been certificated by the CAB in the late 1940s and early 1950s. The subsidy was to ensure services in the small communities, which were not being served by the trunk carriers.

The Airline Deregulation Act of 1978 contains provisions of providing services to small communities. Under the Essential Air Services program (EAS), subsidised air services are being provided by the commuter carriers. Under this scheme, if in a community, which was being provided subsidised service before airline deregulation, the service falls below an essential minimum, then the Department of Transportation is involved in a tendering process. The award for providing the service is given to the commuter airline which wins the competitive bid. The government provides subsidy to the commuter airline. Initially, the EAS program was to end in 1988. However, the Department of Transportation (DOT) approved an extension of the program in 1988 and again in 1997. Reynolds-Feighan (2000) provides an overview of the EAS during the deregulatory period. Table 8.2 gives the number of EAS communities and the types of carriers that serve these communities.

It is clear from the table that the vast majority of the designated EAS communities are receiving services from regional carriers only. For example, in 1997, about 80% of these communities were receiving services only from regional carriers.

Table 8.3 below gives the size distribution of the subsidised EAS communities for 1987, 1994-5 and 1999. Tables 8.2 and 8.3 show us that only a small percentage of EAS communities need subsidised service.

Table 8.2   Number of EAS Communities and the Carriers Serving Them

Year	No. of EAS Communities	Served only by regional carriers	Served only by major and national carriers	Served by regional, major and national carriers
1978	322	112	149	61
1988	327	276	5	40
1989	326	268	4	45
1990	300	243	4	43
1991	505(210)	413	14	44
1992	508(208)	417	8	46
1993	503(205)	423	3	46
1994	501(202)	419	3	44
1995	504(204)	436	6	42
1996	500(202)	399	4	54
1997	499(202)	399	4	55

Note: From 1991 onwards, Alaska communities have been included. These are given in parentheses

Source: Reynolds-Feighan (2000)

Bulk of the communities that receive such service have a population below 30,000. In 1997, the total subsidy payments in 48 contiguous states, Puerto Rico and Alaska amounted to 19.71 million dollars. In total, 92 points were given the subsidies and the average subsidy per point was $214,191. Although not shown here, a comparison of the subsidised EAS communities with the non-subsidised EAS communities reveals that subsidised EAS generally have lower population than the unsubsidised EAS communities.

Table 8.3 Size Distribution of the Subsidised EAS Communities

Population Category	Number subsidised		
	1987	1994-95	1999
Not Available	1	2	1
<5000	8	8	8
5000-9999	14	15	15
10000-19999	29	29	26
20000-29999	17	17	12
30000-49999	16	8	9
50000-99000	7	10	2
100000+	2	1	1

Source: Reynolds-Feighan (2000)

What about the fares that are paid by air passengers travelling to and from these small communities? Detailed data about fares to small communities are not available. The Department of Transportation (1998) study finds that these fares are generally higher than for travellers between large hubs. One factor for the high fare has to do with lack of substitutability. These communities not only suffer from the lack of substitute airports but also from the lack of other modes of transportation (such as railroads).

Did the Non-hub Cities Lose?

If we are to go by the media and newspaper reports, the popular perception is that non-hub cities in general, and small cities in particular, have experienced a deterioration in service. Butler and Huston (1990) examine this question. Their sample consist of 225 airports in the continental US which were not hubs in 1990 but had jet services in 1976. The authors limit the sample size to only airports that had jet services because these were the airports which were likely to lose most from airline deregulation.

Three measures of services are used. These are schedule flexibility, the type of planes flown (jet services may be preferred to propeller-driven

131

planes), most importantly, whether there was convenient service to the destination. The schedule flexibility is measured by the number of non-stop flights.

Contrary to what is reported in the popular press, the results indicated that the travellers to and from non-hub airports had better services in the post-deregulation period than during the period of regulation. The number of non-stop flights went up after deregulation. While it is true that propeller driven services had grown rapidly after deregulation, this had not been followed by a decline in the number of jet services in these non-hubs. In fact, the number of jet services increased.

The study finds that many small cities retained jet services. The number of non-stop destinations increased only modestly even though the number of non-stop services went up by a significant extent. The study also looks at the number of possible daily connections. Most passengers from small cities had to change planes to reach the final destination during the period of deregulation as well. The number of one-stop connections can, therefore, be a better measure of service in this regard. There had been a tremendous increase in one stop connections. Also, the number of on-line connections (as opposed to interline connections) had also increased significantly in ten years from 1978 to 1988. Finally, competition at non-hub airports had also increased. On an average, these cities were served by 3.2 carriers before deregulation. However, after deregulation, this increased to 4.7 carriers.

Airport Delays

The tremendous growth in the airline passenger traffic in the United States after deregulation has resulted in passenger delays at busy airports. Delays are now regularly monitored by the Department of Transportation. Delays are particularly problematic for business passengers.

Since the lack of capacity has been the most important cause of the delays, most previous studies have suggested two basic solutions. These are to increase capacity and better use of capacity (such as peak-load pricing). Hub and spoke operations have added to the problem of delays because in such a system, the airlines land and take off in large numbers during particular times of the day. Many of the busy airports are in the process of increasing capacity. However, the lack of capital of the airport authorities is a major impediment in increasing capacity. Thus, more efficient use of the capacity is also needed.

Rutner, Mundy, and Whitaker (1997) review a number of ways by which the existing capacity can be utilised in a better way. Some of these are being tried out already. First, FAA is trying out a number of different systems of controls. Some systems are meant to reduce runway delays and collisions. Other systems can help to increase the number of flights per hour from a runway.

Second, traffic may be diverted to nearby airports, which have less traffic. In many cases, other airports dot the airports that are capacity-constrained. For example, 100 less busy airports are located within 100 miles of the capacity-constrained airports. Southwest Airlines has used this strategy effectively by avoiding Dallas-Fort Worth and Miami by flying to Dallas-Love Field and Fort Lauderdale respectively.

Third, since hub and spoke operations are a major reason for the delays, relocation of hubs can be a strategy to reduce delays. Delta was able to reduce delays by moving its hub from Chicago to Cincinnati.

Fourth, traffic can be diverted to other modes of transport such as automobiles and buses. Automobiles are most often the most important competitor of the airlines especially for short distances. Finally, peak-load pricing has also been suggested to reduce delays.

Rutner, Mundy and Whitaker surveyed the airport executives to find out what solutions they would prefer. A host of other questions were asked. The response rate from the 100 busiest airports was 70 percent. The respondent airports varied from small to very large airports. As expected, the survey found that larger airports were likely to have more delays due to lack of capacity. 85 percent of the respondents reported that they were in the process of expanding capacity. However, while about 66 percent reported that they were expanding to meet future demand, only 25 percent reported that they were increasing capacity to reduce current delays. The overwhelming majority of the airports in this category were very big airports.

As to the most preferred ways of increasing capacity, the first choice was the reduction of the time interval between take-off and landing through innovations. The second choice was the construction of new runways. There were interesting differences in the responses of the large airports on the one hand and small and medium airports on the other. Large airports favoured the construction of new runways to reduce delays while small and medium airports preferred diversion of traffic from large airports.

Changes in International Aviation and its Effects on the US Airlines

Although airline deregulation has spread to other parts of the world following the lead of the United States in 1978, changes have been slow in coming in the arena of international aviation. What was agreed upon at the Chicago convention in 1944 still largely governs global air transportation. Thus, international air services are still governed by the bilateral agreements approach which is in contrast to trade in goods in which both bilateral and multilateral agreements are common. At the Chicago convention, the US favoured an international aviation policy based on the 'open-skies' philosophy but this was voted down by other countries, which thought that such a policy would lead to the domination by US carriers.

As pointed out by Gourdin (1998), bilaterals are basically treaties between governments rather than between the carriers. These bilateral agreements specify the airports that can be served, the types of aircraft that could be used and the frequency of service. The US has signed a number of "open-skies" agreements in recent years. The years and the countries are given in the table 8.4

Table 8.4 Countries Having 'Open-Skies' Treaties with the United States

Year	Country or Countries
1992	Netherlands
1995	Austria, Belgium, Canada, Czech Republic, Denmark, Finland, Iceland, Luxembourg, Norway, Sweden, Switzerland
1996	Germany, Jordan
1997	Costa Rica, Nicaragua, Honduras, El Salvador, Guatemala, Panama, Taiwan, Brunei, Singapore, New Zealand, Malaysia, Aruba

Source: Gourdin (1998)

The European Union (EU) has been able to achieve limited deregulation. Airlines that are based in the EU countries are now free to serve the airline markets within the EU. Even though it was agreed that the EU would start negotiating air service agreements with other countries, member countries have been reluctant to do so. European Commission has declared that EU countries that signed bilateral agreements after the EU became a single market are in violation of the EU law (Morrocco, 1998). The logic of this argument is that such bilateral agreements discriminate against those EU countries, which have not signed such agreements with the US.

It is expected that in the future, the EU as a single entity will be able to negotiate arrangements with other countries including the United States. If the EU is then treated as a single country, the US will have virtual cabotage rights. Thus, the US may also have to give cabotage rights to these carriers. Strategic alliances between EU members and non-members may be problematic because these are not governed by European regulations.

Even though many national carriers have now been privatised, some others have not been. Many of these airlines are running at a loss and are being subsidised by the government. However, non-economic factors are also at play in many such cases. A national airline is seen as a symbol of national pride. In many developing countries, it is a major employer. The provision of quality air service may be looked upon as one of the functions of the government. In practice, however, the quality of service in many such national carriers has declined substantially raising doubts about whether this objective is being fulfilled. None of the US airlines, on the other hand, belonged to the government. Thus, when major airlines like Pan Am and Eastern failed, the government did not try to bail them out.

Effects on Earnings of Airline Employees

In an influential study, Hendricks, Fueille and Szerezen (1980) find that before deregulation, workers in the airline industry received higher than average national wages. This could be attributed to the high level of unionisation and characteristics of the labour force in the sector.

Card (1996) uses a number of data sources to study the impact of airline deregulation on the structure of labour earnings. All data sources show that the wage premium earned by the airline workers during the regulatory period was rather modest. Census data for 1980 and 1990 indicate that during the ten-year period, there was a ten percent decline in the relative earnings of the airline workers. Union contract data for pilots, flight attendants and mechanics showed a similar decline as did the data for displaced worker surveys. The study also finds that the inter-firm wage inequality increased after deregulation.

Compared to many other industries in the United States, the labour market in the airline industry is highly unionised. Hirsch and Macpherson (2000) study how labour earnings have changed in the deregulatory era. If it is found that labour earnings have not changed much after deregulation, one can probably conclude that either labour's rent (rents are defined as payments to labour over and above the long-run opportunity costs) and union strength have either been maintained or labour never had earned such rents before and after deregulation.

Studies, which look at data for the period after deregulation through to the late 1980s suggest that to be the case (see for example, Card, 1986 and the survey by Winston, 1993). This is in contrast to the trucking industry where deregulation was followed by a decline in unionisation, a fall in the union wages and to a lesser extent, a fall in the non-union wages. Card (1986) is of the view that workers were not earning such rents even before airline deregulation. Hendricks (1994), on the other hand, has the opposite conclusion. He argues that the relatively little change in the wages was a reflection of the fact that a concentrated product market and union strength were the explanation for the persistence of higher wages in the airline industry even after deregulation.

The results of the earlier studies are to be contrasted with that of the later studies such as Hirsch and Macpherson (2000). Hirsch and Macpherson find that during the late 1980s and the 1990s, there had been a significant fall in the relative earnings advantage (that is, when the earnings of the airline workers are compared to those of other workers) of the airline employees. Hirsch and Macpherson calculate the wage premiums for the following four categories: (a) pilots, (b) flight attendants, (c) mechanics, (d) fleet service (ramp) workers and (e) ticket and reservation agents and traffic, shipping, and receiving clerks. For these four categories of workers, comparison groups are identified in other occupations.

Wage premiums were found to be modest for other three categories but not for pilots. Hirsch and Macpherson show that rents that were being received by the workers can be explained by the presence of unions. The period of deregulation has also been marked by a higher pay gap between the union and non-union workers. These rents increased immediately after deregulation as a result of a tremendous increase in the number of passengers and not a very elastic supply of labour. Since the mid-1980s, these rents have fallen first for the non-union workers and then, for the union workers. The bargaining power of the unions declined during the late 1980s and the early 1990s due to the poor financial performance of the airlines. Since then, the financial position of the airlines has become better leading to an improved bargaining power of the unions. However, the airlines are beset by lack of trust between the management and the employees.

Effects on Profits of the Airlines

One of the objectives of the regulation of airlines by the CAB had been to regulate fares so that the airline industry would get a 'fair rate of return'. One fear of deregulation had been that deregulation would lead to destructive competition because of cutthroat competition which would ultimately lead to the development of a less competitive structure in the airline industry. Indeed, in a study of profits of the airlines after the period immediately following deregulation, Brenner, Leet and Schott (1985) find that the profits were the lowest during the period after deregulation. The low growth of the economy and rising fuel costs during the period immediately following deregulation might have been partially responsible for the decline in profits since the fares declined during the same period.

In another study, Gomez-Ibanez, Clinton and Pickrell (1983) estimate an air travel demand model. Then, they calculate what the demand would have been had the economy grown at the normal (long run) rate. They also calculate the additional costs associated with additional passengers with such normal growth. In estimating the costs, they adjust fuel costs for the abnormal increase, i.e., in their cost estimates, such fuel costs were taken into account if fuel costs increases were steady. After such adjustments, they found that deregulation did not have much to do with the fall in profitability. The slow growth of the economy and the increase in fuel costs were the main reasons for the relatively lower profits in 1979 and losses in 1980 and 1981.

Van Scyoc (1989) uses a regression model explaining the net profit margin of the airlines using annual data for the period 1964-86. The explanatory variables included fuel, wage, interest, GNP, yield, a dummy for the period of deregulation and three quarterly dummies. The results show that the coefficient for the dummy variable for deregulation was not significant whereas the coefficients for fuel, wage, GNP and quarterly dummies were highly significant. Thus, the author's conclusion is that fuel costs, wage and the low growth of the economy, rather than deregulation, were responsible for the low profit margin. However, the relatively high numbers of explanatory variables and the low number of observations in the study meant that the degrees of freedom were rather low and much credence may not be placed on the results of the study.

Effects on Labour Productivity

Meyer and Strong (1992) contend that deregulation has been accompanied by rapid entry and exit. Deregulation led to an increase in labour productivity and a fall in real average compensation of the employees during the first ten years of deregulation. In the authors' opinion, the financial performance, industry structure and concentration, problems of congestion and public infrastructure had more to do with matters of public policy than with airline deregulation. In a number of ways, the government still does have a lot of control over the industry. For example, even now the government controls bulk of the decisions relating to the industry's infrastructure in airports and airways. Meyer and Strong also feel that the consumers had not got the full potential benefits of deregulation because the government had not enforced the antitrust laws in ways, which would have promoted more competition.

The Bureau of Labor Statistics estimates that the employment in commercial aviation in the United States increased 413 percent between 1958 and 1996. The number of jobs increased from 165,000 in 1958 to 847,000 in 1996 (Goodman, 2000). If we compare the growth rate of employment for other modes of transportation with that of other modes, we see that the increase had been a lot slower for the other modes of transportation. Between 1958 and 1996, output (as measured mostly by passenger-miles and cargo ton-miles) increased by more than 1,800 percent. However, the growth of output had not been uniform. The output grew at an average rate of 10.6 percent a year from 1958 to 1978 but the growth rate fell to 5.5 percent a year between 1978 and 1996. Between 1986 and 1996, the growth rate was even lower at five percent.

This increase in output could have been attributed to an increase in the capital input in many other industries. However, we cannot say the same about the airline industry, which remains a labour-intensive service industry. Thus, it is clear that there had been a massive increase in the productivity of labour during this period. As in the case of output, the growth in the labour force had not been uniform. The growth rate had mirrored the growth rate of output and had fallen considerably in the recent decades. The growth rate was 4.6 percent between 1958 and 1978, 4.1 percent between 1978 and 1996 and 2.2 percent between 1990 and 1996 (Goodman, 2000). In recent years, the job growth rate has been much faster for cargo than for passengers. The tremendous growth of air couriers has been an important factor in this growth.

The growth of productivity also had not been uniform. However, productivity almost continuously increased on a per-employee basis since 1947 (Goodman, 2000). The exceptions were the following years: 1980, 1981, 1988 and 1991. This was due to the recessions and the consequent fall in the load factors. Productivity did increase during the regulatory period as well. It was mainly due to the increase in the size and speed of the aircraft. Introduction of jet engines was an important milestone for the airlines. Increase in the size of the aircraft increased the productivity of the crewmembers because as the size of the plane increases, the number of crewmembers does not increase proportionately.

The average number of seats in an aircraft carrying passengers increased to 165 passenger seats in 1983. Since then, however, it fell to 152 in 1996. The increases in the number of seats can increase productivity only if the load factor does not fall. Indeed, the increase in the load factor had been much more significant during the period of deregulation. While the load factor increased about 0.2 percent per year from 1958 to 1978, the rate of growth jumped to 0.7 per year from 1978 to 1996. One important reason for the increase in the load factor is the hub and spoke system. Deregulation has also enabled the airlines to use much smaller aeroplanes on routes where the demand is low. This has also contributed to the increase in the load factor. However, Goodman finds that the average number of passengers carried per aircraft mile increased from 90 in 1978 to 103 in 1996. This also contributed to the increase in productivity. During the post-deregulation period, other factors, which increased productivity, were also at work.

First, the computer reservation system became much more widespread. Computer reservation system reduces the demand for ground staff. Second, when price war broke out following deregulation, the major airlines were able to quickly reduce the number of employees. The same thing happened when a recession broke out. However, further gains in productivity can come only from new cost saving techniques, which may emerge in the future.

Effects of Frequent Fliers

We took a brief look at the issue of frequent flier programs in chapter 1. Here, we concentrate on the studies on frequent flier programs in the US where it is most popular. One way of viewing frequent flyer is to think of them as quantity discounts. Such quantity discounts are quite common in other industries. 'Buy one pair of shoes and get another pair free' or 'Buy a pair of glasses and get a second pair free' are examples. As Borenstein (1992) notes, if marginal cost is below average cost, quantity discounts help to cover total costs, whereas such discounts reduce inefficiency if marginal price is above marginal cost.

As a passenger builds up mileage on a single airline, the marginal value of the reward increases. Thus, she/he is likely to choose the airline that he/she is likely to fly in the future. The passenger is likely to choose that airline which offers many flights from the her/his home airport. Business passengers are likely to be targeted more by frequent flier programs. As Levine (1987) points out, business passengers whose air tickets are paid for by the employers, are likely to choose an airline for which they get frequent flier benefits rather than the one with lowest price and/or reduced travel time. As pointed out by Borenstein (1992), a General Accounting Office survey of the travel agents shows that indeed more than half of the business passengers almost always chose flights that matched their frequent flier programs. This untaxed fringe benefit adds to the business passengers' benefits but it is a burden on the taxpayers in general and the government in particular. In principle, it is possible for the employer to treat the estimated frequent flier miles as benefits and thus, adjust other salary and benefits accordingly. However, this still does not reduce the burden on the taxpayers and the government. Morrison and Winston (1990) propose a tax on frequent flier benefits but realise that it is unlikely to happen because it is going to be unpopular and difficult. The taxing authority will have to distinguish between awards earned for personal travel and business travel. There are other complications. Frequent fliers are no longer restricted to national boundaries. With worldwide alliances among airlines, passengers are able to use the frequent flier benefits outside their own countries – this makes taxing the frequent flier benefits even more difficult.

There are analogous schemes for the travel agents. These are called travel agent commission overrides (TACOs). The majority of the travel agents receive higher commission rates from at least one airline for diverting traffic to that airline (Borenstein, 1992). Both Borenstein (1992) and Levine (1987) argue that the dominant airline in an area is able to use TACOs very effectively.

Even though the situation may seem comparable to the case of other products and services because the salespersons for different brand names often also receive such commissions, there are subtle differences. Most passengers view travel agents as unbiased sources of information. They view that the travel agents have only the passengers' welfare in mind. Thus, they are not able to detect the biases that the travel agents have. Even if they are aware of such biases, passengers simply do not have perfect information and thus, have to rely on the travel agents. After deregulation, there have been many choices that are often available and fares and seat availability keep changing constantly. Use of the internet for purchasing tickets has added another dimension to the issue. Of course, travel agents as well as the airlines could be contacted through the internet.

Banerjee and Summers (1987) argue that the effect of frequent flier programs and TACOs is to lower cross-elasticity of demand between products. This reduces the incentive to competitive price cuts. Thus, these programs lead to market division and tacit price collusion.

Effects on Safety

The concern with safety has been associated with the fear that with deregulation, the replacement of jet services by commuter services can lead to less safety. Almost all studies about airline safety, which have used data for jet services to find that the safety record of jet services has improved after deregulation. In fact, safety had been increasing for a long time before airline deregulation. However, small communities have lost jet service and they are being serviced by commuter airlines. Oster and Zorn (1989) find that commuter airlines had a higher fatality rate than that of trunk and local service airlines. A good review of the airline safety debate is found in Rose (1992).

Figure 8.1 gives the annual number of fatal accidents per million aircraft miles from 1938 to 1999. It shows that there had been an almost continuous fall in this measure especially since 1938.

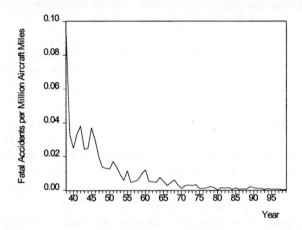

Figure 8.1   Fatal Accidents per Million Aircraft Miles, 1938-99
Source: Air Transport Association (2000)

A related measure is the passenger fatalities per million aircraft miles. Figure 8.2 shows this measure from 1932 to 1999. The figure shows wider fluctuations in this measure than the other measure. During the early part of the 1940s, there was a substantial increase in the passenger fatality per million aircraft miles. Since then, in spite of the fluctuations, there has been a perceptible fall in the measure.

Using monthly data from January 1966 to December 1989, Kanafani and Keeler (1990) study whether there had been any change in the trend of safety in the post-deregulation period. They run the following exponential (non-linear) regression:

$$DPM = \exp(a_1 + a_2 + a_3\ T.D) + u \tag{8.5}$$

where DPM stands for fatalities per revenue passenger-mile in a regularly scheduled service, T is a time trend (taking the value of 1 in January 1966, a value of 2 in February 1996 and so on) and D is the dummy variable having a value of 0 before January, 1979 and a value of 1 thereafter. a_3 shows the shift in the trend in the change of fatalities after deregulation.

142

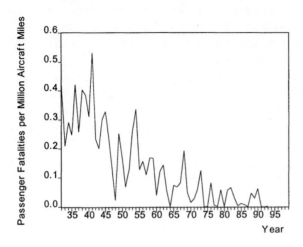

Figure 8.2 Passenger Fatalities per Million Aircraft Miles, 1932-99
Source: Air Transport Association (2000)

Because of the problem of heteroscedasticity, the equation is estimated by the method of nonlinear generalised weighted least squares. The results show that a3 is not significant implying that there had been no change in the trend towards fatality. In other words, deregulation did not have any effect on the airline industry's trend towards improved safety.

Safety, Profitability and Load Factor

In this section, we perform the block Granger block non-causality tests (see Granger, 1969) between profitability, safety and the load factor. The results are from Sinha (2000). A study by Adrangi, Chow and Raffiee (1997) also employs Granger causality tests between profitability and safety. However, there are a number of differences between the present study and the study by Adrangi, Chow and Raffiee. First, they do not take load factor into account in their causality tests. Thus, while their tests are confined to bivariate causality tests, we perform both bivariate and multivariate causality tests.

Second, to take airline deregulation into account, they split the data into two periods, pre-deregulation and post-deregulation periods and

143

performed causality tests separately for these two periods. Since their data end in 1994 (safety data are up to 1992 only), they are able to use only 14 years of post deregulation data to test for Granger causality! This time period is too short to get any meaningful results. In our view, a more satisfactory way of dealing with the event of airline deregulation is to treat airline deregulation as a form of structural break. Our causality tests use data for the whole period – but, we treat airline deregulation as a structural break in our causality tests.

Third, our measures of profitability are different from the measures that they use. We also normalise the measures of profitability as they do. However, while we use operating profit per passenger and net operating profit per passenger, they use operating profit and net operating profit divided by total revenue.

The Granger block non-causality test can be described as follows. Consider the augmented vector autoregressive model:

$$z_t = a_0 + a_1 t + \sum_{i=1}^{p} \phi_i z_{t-i} + \Psi w_t + u_t \qquad (8.6)$$

where z_t is an m x 1 vector of jointly determined (endogenous) variables, t is a linear time trend, w_t is q x 1 vector of exogenous variables, and u_t is an m x 1 vector of unobserved disturbances. Let $z_t = (z'_{1t}, z'_{2t})'$, where z'_{1t} and z'_{2t} are m_1 x 1 and m_2 x 1 subsets of z_t, and $m = m_1 + m_2$. We can now have the block decomposition of (3) as follows:

$$z_{1t} = a_{10} + a_{11}t + \sum_{i=1}^{p} \phi_{i,\,11} z_{1,t-i} + \sum_{i=1}^{p} \phi_{i,\,12} z_{2,t-i} + \Psi_1 w_t + u_{1t} \qquad (8.7)$$

$$z_{2t} = a_{20} + a_{21}t + \sum_{i=1}^{p} \phi_{i,\,21} z_{1,t-i} + \sum_{i=1}^{p} \phi_{i,\,22} z_{2,t-i} + \Psi_2 w_t + u_{2t} \qquad (8.8)$$

The hypothesis that the subset z_{2t} do not 'Granger cause' z_{1t} is given by H_G: $\phi_{12} = 0$ where $\phi_{12} = (\phi_{1,12}, \phi_{2,12} \ldots, \phi_{1p,12})$.

However, before we perform such tests, we have to ensure that the variables involved are stationary. If the variables are non-stationary in their levels, but stationary in their first differences, then cointegration tests can be performed. If the variables are cointegrated, causality tests can still be performed but an error correction form needs to be used.

We use Phillips-Perron (1988) test because the test is well suited for analysing time series whose differences may follow mixed ARMA (p,q) processes of unknown order in that it the test statistic incorporates a nonparametric allowance for serial correlation and heteroscedasticity in testing the regression. Consider the following equation:

$$\tilde{y}_t = \tilde{c}_0 + \tilde{c}_1 y_{t-1} + \tilde{c}_2 (t - T/2) + v_t \qquad (8.9)$$

where T is the number of observations and v_t is the error term. The null hypothesis of a unit root is: $\tilde{c}_1 = 1$. We can drop the trend term to test the stationarity of a variable without the trend.

All data are from the Air Transport Association (2000). The annual data are for the period from 1947 to 1998. The variables are defined as follows. Two measures of air safety are used. These are fatal accidents per million aircraft miles (FAPMAM) and passenger fatalities per million aircraft miles (PFPMAM). Two measures of profitability are used. These are real operating profit per passenger (ROPPP) and real net operating profit per passenger. Finally, load factor (LF) is the system-wide load factor.

The results of the Phillips-Perron unit root tests are given in table 8.5. The results show that while FAPMAM, PFPMAM, ROPPP and RNOPPP are all stationary, LF is not. We use critical values at the 5 percent level of significance. Since LF is not stationary, we can use the growth rate of LF (which we call GLF) in our causality analysis provided that GLF is stationary. The table also shows that GLF is stationary. Thus, in the causality tests, we use GLF along with other variables.

Our causality analysis takes airline deregulation into account as a structural break. Since the Airline Deregulation Act was passed in 1978, we take 1979 to be the year of the structural break. The structural break is taken into account as an exogenous variable.

Table 8.5 Phillips-Perron (PP) Unit Root Tests (Truncation lag = 3[*])

Variable	PP Test Statistic[**]	Critical Value
FAPMAN	$T_\mu = -3.5383$	-2.9190
FAPMAM	$T_\tau = -4.6078$	-3.4987
PFPMAM	$T_\mu = -5.0047$	-2.9190
PFPMAM	$T_\tau = -7.4327$	-3.4987
ROPPP	$T_\mu = -3.2766$	-2.9190
ROPPP	$T_\tau = -4.0352$	-3.4987
RNOPPP	$T_\mu = -3.6222$	-2.9190
RNOPPP	$T_\tau = -4.4117$	-3.4987
LF	$T_\mu = -1.4291$	-2.9190
LF	$T_\tau = -1.6990$	-3.4987
GLF	$T_\mu = -6.9432$	-2.9202
GLF	$T_\tau = -6.9729$	-3.5005

[*]The truncation lag of 3 was determined using the Schwert Criterion. The truncation lag = integer [$4(T/100)^{1/4}$] where T stands for the number of observations.

[**] T_μ and T_τ and are test statistics (1) with drift and no trend and (2) with drift and trend respectively. Critical values at 5% level are simulated from Mackinnon (1991).

Source: Sinha (2000)

Since we have two measures of profitability and two measures of safety, and the growth of load factor is also included in the causality tests, a large number of causality tests need to be conducted. In all causality tests, we take into account the structural break due to airline deregulation. The results of multivariate and bivariate causality tests are given in table 8.6.

Table 8.6 Multivariate and Bivariate Granger Block Causality Tests

Cause	Effect	Test Stat.(*)	Probability(**)
ROPPP, GLOAD	FAPMM	12.25(3)	.057(6)
ROPPP, GLOAD	PFMAM	11.77(3)	.067(6)
RNOPPP, GLOAD	FAPMM	13.70(3)	.033(6)
RNOPPP, GLOAD	PFMAM	12.71(3)	.048(6)
ROPPP	FAPMM	3.97(3)	.265(3)
ROPPP	PFMAM	5.67(3)	.129(3)
RNOPPP	FAPMM	1.66(3)	.647(3)
RNOPPP	PFMAM	2.01(3)	.570(3)
ROPPP	GLOAD	19.10(3)	.000(3)
GLOAD	ROPPP	5.66(3)	.129(3)
RNOPPP	GLOAD	20.57(3)	.000(3)
GLOAD	RNOPPP	3.86(3)	.277(3)

Note: The test statistic indicates the chi-square value. The probability refers to the probability of accepting the null hypothesis of no causality
*indicates the number of lags which was determined by using the Akaike Information Criterion (AIC)
**indicates the degrees of freedom of the chi-square distribution

Source: Sinha (2000)

The results show that there is some evidence that profitability and the growth of load factor Granger caused fatalities/accidents. The evidence is stronger when real net operating profit per passenger (RNOPPP) is used. Bivariate causality tests between measures of profitability and the measures of safety show that there was no evidence that profitability Granger caused fatalities/accidents.   This leads us to conclude that the growth of load factor and not profitability contributed to the Granger causality. We also conduct Granger causality tests between the growth rate of load factor and profitability.   There is strong evidence that the causality flowed from profitability to the growth of load factor. This is true for both measures of profitability. There is no evidence of reverse causality that the growth of load factor Granger caused profitability.

The Issue of Privatisation

Privatisation of airports has been an important issue in the United States. After cargo and passenger traffic deregulation, there has been an increasing pressure on privatisation. A lively controversy has emerged in which not only economists but also political scientists and other social scientists have taken part. In the United States, most of the airports are owned and operated by the local city governments.

A survey by Rutner, Mundy and Whitaker (1997) looks at the sources of funding of the busiest airports. Based on the response of 70 airports, it is found that as a single entity, federal government is the most important source of funding of the airports providing 35 percent of total funding. States and local municipalities provide 39 percent of the funding while airports themselves raise the remaining 26 percent by various schemes such as passenger facility charges (PFCs). Sources other than the federal government are more important sources of funding for capital expansion of these airports.

Conclusions

Most studies find that most consumers have gained from airline deregulation in the form of lower airfares and in some cases, better flight frequencies. In general, deregulation has benefited air travellers from large airports have benefited more. In many cases, the smaller airports have lost jet service. Studies on the profitability of the airlines, which were done mostly in the 1980s, find that deregulation did not have much impact on profitability. Studies also find an increase in concentration after deregulation. Some commentators have argued for re-regulation of the airline industry. However, re-regulation does not appear to be the right policy to adopt.

Bibliography

Adrangi, B., Chow, G. and Raffiee, K. (1997), 'Airline Deregulation, Safety and Profitability in the U.S', *Transportation Journal*, vol. 46, pp. 44-52.

Air Transport Association (2000), *Airline Handbook*, http://www.air-transport.org.

Airline Industry Investigation (1947), Hearings pursuant to Senate Resolution before the Committee on Interstate and Foreign Commerce, 1st and 2nd Sessions, House Document Nos. 46 and 95.

Airport Survey (1945), 76th Congress, 1st Session, House Document No. 87.

Alamdri, F.E. and Morrell, P. (1997), 'Airline Labour Cost Reduction: Post-liberalisation Experience in the USA and Europe', *Journal of Air Transport Management*, vol. 3, pp. 53-66.

Al-Jazzaf, M. (1999), 'Impact of Privatisation in Airlines Performance', Journal *of Air Transport Management*, vol. 5, pp. 45-52.

Anonymous (2000a), 'Airline Alliances – Dangerous Liaisons', *Economist*, vol. 356, issue 8, p. 61.

Anonymous (2000b), 'Angel Stops to Find its Wings', *Airfinance Journal*, July/August, p. 13.

Anonymous (2000c), 'Garuda Takes off After Whirlwind Restructuring Programme', *Asiamoney*, September, pp. 12-13.

Anonymous (2000d), 'Air Canada Wins the War, Acquires Canadian Airlines', *Logistics Management and Distribution Report*, vol. 39, issue 2, p. 65.

Anonymous (2000e), 'Facts and Figures', *Air Transport World*, vol. 37, issue 6, p. 90.

Armstrong, M, Cowan, S. and Vickers, J. (1994), *Regulatory Reform: An Economic Analysis and British Experience*, MIT Press, Cambridge, MA.

Averch, H. and Johnson, L. (1962), 'Behavior of the Firm under Regulatory Constraint', *American Economic Review*, vol. 52, pp. 1052-69.

Bailey, E.E. and Panzar, J.C. (1981), 'The Contestability of Airline Markets during the Transition to Deregulation', *Law and Contemporary Problems*, vol. 44, pp. 125-45.

Bailey, E.E., Graham, D.R. and Kaplan, D. (1985), *Deregulating the Airlines*, MIT Press, Cambridge, MA.

Bain, J.S. (1949), 'A Note on Pricing in Monopoly and Oligopoly', *American Economic Review*, vol. 39, pp. 448-64.

Bain, J.S. (1959), *Industrial Organization*, John Wiley, New York.

Baldwin, J.R. (1975), *The Regulatory Agency and the Public Corporation: The Canadian Air Transport Industry*, Ballinger Publishing Company, Cambridge, MA.

Banerjee, A. and Summers, L. (1987), 'On Frequent-Flyer Programs and Other Loyalty-Inducing Economic Arrangements', Harvard Institute of Economic Research Discussion Paper No. 1337, September.

Barrett, S.D. (1999), 'Peripheral Market Entry, Product Differentiation, Supplier Rents and Sustainability in the Deregulated European Airline Market – a Case Study', *Journal of Air Transport Management*, vol. 5, pp. 21-30.

Barrett, S.D. (2000), 'Airport Competition in the Deregulated European Aviation Market', *Journal of Air Transport Management*, vol. 6, pp. 13-27.

Baumol, W.J. (1982), 'Contestable Markets: An Uprising in the Theory of Industrial Structure', *American Economic Review*, vol. 72, pp. 1-15.

Baumol, W.J., Panzar, J.C. and Willig, R.D. (1982), *Contestable Markets and the Theory of Industry Structure*, Harcourt Brace Jovanovich, New York.

Baumol, W.J. and Willig, R.D. (1986), 'Contestability: Developments Since the Book', Research Report #86-01, New York University.

Becker, G. (1983), 'A Theory of Competition among Pressure Groups for Political Influence', *Quarterly Journal of Economics*, vol. 98, pp. 371-400.

Berge, S. (1951), 'Subsidies and Competition as Factors in Air Transport Policy', *Journal of Air Law and Commerce*, vol. 18, pp. 7-10.

Berge, S. (1955), 'Competition to the Extent Necessary', *Journal of Air Law and Commerce*, vol. 22, pp. 127-30.

Berry, S.T. (1990), 'Airport Presence as Product Differentiation', *American Economic Review*, vol. 80, pp. 394-99.

Borenstein, S. (1989), 'Hubs and High Fares: Dominance and Market Power in the U.S. Airline Industry', *Rand Journal of Economics*, vol. 20, pp. 344-65.

Borenstein, S. (1992), 'The Evolution of U.S. Airline Competition', *Journal of Economic Perspectives*, vol. 6, pp. 45-73.

Bibliography

Bowen, J.T. Jr. and Leinbach, T. R. (1996), 'Development and Liberalization: The Airline Industry in ASEAN', in G.C. Hufbauer and C. Findlay (eds.).

Brenner, M.A., Leet, J.O. and Schott, E. (1985), *Airline Deregulation*, Eno Foundation, Westport, Connecticut.

Breyer, S.G. and Stein, L.R. (1982), 'Airline Deregulation: The Anatomy of Reform', in R.W. Poole Jr. (ed.), *Instead of Regulation: Alternatives to Federal Regulatory Agencies*, Lexington Books, Lexington, MA.

Briand, S. and Kelvin, A. (1998), 'Assessment of the Regulatory Reform in the European Airlines', *International Journal of Transport Economics*, vol. 25, pp. 3-17.

Brogden, S. (1968), *Australia's Two-Airline Policy*, Melbourne University Press, Melbourne.

Bureau of Transport and Communications Economics (1991a), *A New Era in Australian Aviation: Conference Papers*, Australian Government Publishing Service, Canberra.

Bureau of Transport and Communications Economics (1991b), *Deregulation of Domestic Aviation: The First Year*, Report 73, Australian Government Publishing Service, Canberra.

Bureau of Transport Economics (1985), *Competition and Regulation in Domestic Aviation: Submission to Independent Review*, Occasional Paper 72, Australian Government Publishing Service, Canberra.

Bureau of Transport Economics (2000), Australia, http://www.dotrs.gov.au /bte/genpub/indicats/paxsec/airfares.htm.

Butler, R.V. and Huston, J.H. (1990), 'Airline Service to Non-Hub Airports Ten Years after Deregulation', *Logistics and Transportation Review*, vol. 26, pp. 3-16.

Button, K. (1996), 'Liberalizing European Aviation: Is There an Empty Core Problem', *Journal of Transport Economics and Policy*, vol. 30, pp. 275-91.

Button, K. (1997), 'Developments in the European Union: Lessons for the Pacific Asia Region', in C. Findlay, C.L. Sien and K. Singh (eds.), *Asia Pacific Air Transport: Challenges and Policy Reforms*, Institute of Southeast Asian Studies, Singapore.

Button, K. and Johnson, K. (1998), 'Incremental versus Trend-Break Change in Airline Regulation', *Transportation Journal*, vol. 37, pp. 25-34.

Captain, P.F. and Sickles, R.C. (1997), 'Competition and Market Power in the European Airline Industry', *Managerial and Decision Economics*, vol. 18, pp. 209-225.

Card, D. (1986), 'The Impact of Deregulation on the Employment and Wages of the Airline Mechanics', *Industrial and Labor Relations Review*, vol. 39, pp. 527-38.

Card, D. (1996), 'Deregulation and Labor Earnings in the Airline Industry', NBER Working Paper No. 5687, July.

Caves, D.W., Christensen, L.R. and Tretheway, M.W. (1984), 'Economies of Density versus Economies of Scale: Why Trunk and Local Service Airline Costs Differ', *Rand Journal of Economics*, vol. 15, pp. 471-89.

Caves, R.E. (1962), *Air Transport and its Regulators*, Harvard University Press, Cambridge, MA.

Civil Aeronautics Board, Docket 2068, *American Airlines, Inc. Acquisition of Mid-Continental Airlines*, 19 April, 1946.

Civil Aeronautics Board (1974), *Domestic Route System: Analysis and Policy Recommendations*, Washington, DC, October.

Civil Aeronautics Board (1976), *Domestic Passenger-Fare Investigation*: *January 1970 to December 1974*, Washington, DC.

Civil Aviation Authority (1995), *CAP 654 The Single Aviation Market: Progress So Far*, Civil Aviation Authority, London.

Commission of the European Communities (1996), *Impact of the Third Package of Air Transport Liberalization Measures*.

Crane, J.B. (1944), 'The Economics of Air Transportation', *Harvard Business Review*, vol. 22, pp. 495-509.

Davies, G.D. (1971), 'The Efficiency of Public versus Private Firms: The Case of Australia's Two Airlines', *Journal of Law and Economics*, vol. 14, pp. 149-65.

Davies, G.D. (1977), 'Property Rights and Economic Efficiency – the Australian Airlines Revisited', *Journal of Law and Economics*, vol. 20, pp. 223-26.

Demsetz, H. (1968), 'Why Regulate Utilities?', *Journal of Law and Economics*, vol. 11, pp. 55-65.

Department of Economic Affairs (1998), Ministry of Finance, *Economic Survey*, Government of India, Press, New Delhi.

Department of Economic Affairs (2000), Ministry of Finance, *Economic Survey*, Government of India, Press, New Delhi.

Bibliography

Department of Transport (1979), *Domestic Air Transport Policy Review: Report and Appendices*, Australian Government Publishing Service, Canberra.

Department of Transport and Communications (1991), *1990-91 Annual Report*, Australian Government Publishing Service, Canberra.

Department of Transportation (1998), *Rural Air Fare Study*, US Department of Transportation, Washington, DC.

Douglas, E.J. and Cunningham, L.J. (1992), 'Airline Deregulation in Australia: Lessons Learnt and Opportunities Lost', Working Paper, Bond University.

Douglas, G.W. and Miller III, J.C. (1974), *Economic Regulation of Domestic Air Transport: Theory and Policy*, The Brookings Institution, Washington, DC.

Eads, G., Nerlove, M. and Raduchel, W. (1969), 'A Long-Run Cost Function for the Local Service Airline Industry: An Experiment in Non-Linear Estimation', *Review of Economics and Statistics*, vol. 51, pp. 258-70.

Feldman, J.M. (2000), 'Alliance Costs Start Building', *Air Transport World*, vol. 37, issue 6, pp. 41-48.

Findlay, C. (1996), 'The Trans-Tasman Single Aviation Market', *Journal of Transport Economics and Policy*, vol. 30, pp. 329-34.

Flint, P. (1998), 'Transborder Twist', *Air Transport World*, vol. 35, issue 5, pp. 77-79.

Forsyth, P. J. (1979), 'The Two-Airline Policy: Its Results and Future', *The Australian Quarterly*, vol. 51, 62-73.

Forsyth, P.J. (1991), 'Regulation and Deregulation of Australia's Domestic Airline Industry', in K. Button (ed.), *Airline Deregulation: International Experiences*, New York University Press, New York.

Forsyth, P.J. and Hocking, R.D. (1980), 'Property Rights and Efficiency in a Regulated Environment: The Case of Australian Airlines', *Economic Record*, vol. 56, pp. 182-85.

Gallaghar, T. and Jenkins, D. (1996), 'Going when the Price is Right', *Airfinance Journal*, February, pp. 38-40.

Gill, F.W. and Bates, G.L. (1949), *Airline Competition*, Harvard University Press, Cambridge, MA.

Goldberg, S. (1994), *Troubled Skies: Crisis, Competition and Control in Canada's Airline Industry*, McGraw Hill Ryerson, Toronto.

153

Gomez-Ibanez, J.A., Clinton, O.V. and Pickrell, D.H. (1983), 'Airline Deregulation: What is Behind the Recent Losses?', *Journal of Policy Analysis and Management*, vol. 2, Fall, pp. 74-89.
Good, D.H., Roller, L.H. and Sickles, R.C. (1993), 'U.S. Airline Deregulation: Implications for European Transport', *Economic Journal*, vol. 103, pp. 1028-41.
Good, D.H., Roller, L.H. and Sickles, R.C. (1995), 'Airline Efficiency Differences and between Europe and the US: Implications for Pace of EC Integration and Domestic Regulation', *European Journal of Operations Research*, vol. 80, pp. 508-18.
Goodman, W.C. (2000), 'Transportation by Air: Job Growth Moderates from Stellar Rates', *Monthly Labor Review*, vol. 123, pp. 34-47.
Graham, B. (1997a), 'Liberalization, Regional Economic Development and the Geography of Demand for Air Transport', *Journal of Transport Geography*, vol. 6, pp. 87-104.
Graham, B. (1997b), 'Air Transport Liberalization in the European Union: An Assessment', *Regional Studies*, vol. 31, pp. 807-812.
Graham, D.R. and Kaplan, D.P. (1982), 'Airlines Deregulation is Working', Regulation, vol. 6, pp. 26-32.
Graham, D.R., Kaplan, D.P. and Sibley, D.S. (1983), 'Efficiency and Competition in the Airline Industry', *The Bell Journal of Economics*, vol. 14, pp. 118-138.
Granger, C.W.J (1969), 'Investigating Causal Relations by Econometric Models and Cross Spectral Methods', *Econometrica*, vol. 37, pp. 424-38.
Green, H (1990), 'What Can We Learn from America: Can the Fliers Stay Airborne?', *JASSA: Journal of the Australian Securities Association*, no. 4, pp. 23-25.
Gourdin, K.N. (1998), 'U.S. International Aviation Policy into the New Millennium: Meeting the Global Challenge', *Transportation Journal*, vol. 37, pp. 13-19.
Harberger, A. (1978), 'On the Use of Distributional Weights in Social Cost Benefit Analysis', *Journal of Political Economy*, vol. 86, 87-120.
Hendricks, W. (1994), 'Deregulation and Labor Earnings', *Journal of Labor Research*, vol. 15, pp. 207-34.
Hendricks, W., Feuille, P. and Szerezen, C. (1980), 'Regulation, Deregulation and, and Collective Bargaining in Airlines', *Industrial and Labor Relations Review*, vol. 34, pp. 67-81.

Bibliography

Hirsch, B.T. and Macpherson, D.A. (2000), 'Earnings, Rents, and Competition in the Airline Labor Market', *Journal of Labor Economics*, vol. 18, pp. 125-55.

Hocking, D.M. and Haddon-Cave, C.P. (1951), *Air Transport in Australia*, Angus and Robertson, Sydney.

Hocking, R.D. and Forsyth, P.J. (1982), 'The Australian Two-Airline Policy: A Case Study', in L.R. Webb and A.H. Allan (eds.) *Industrial Economics: Australian Studies*, George Allen and Unwin, Sydney.

Holcroft, W. (1981), *Domestic Air Fares: Report of the Independent Public Inquiry, Volumes I-III*, Australian Government Publishing Service, Canberra.

Hufbauer, G.C. and Findlay, C. (eds.) (1996), *Flying High: Liberalizing Civil Aviation in the Asia Pacific*, Institute for International Economics, Washington, DC.

Humphreys, B. (1996), 'The UK Civil Aviation Authority and European Air Services Liberalisation', *Journal of Transport Economics and Policy*, vol. 3, pp. 213-20.

Hurdle, G.J., Johnson R.L., Joskow, A.S., Werden, G. J. and Williams, M. A. (1989), 'Concentration, Potential Entry, and Performance in the Airline Industry', *Journal of Industrial Economics*, vol. 38, pp. 119-139.

Jaggi, G. and Morgan, G. (1996) 'Recent Civil Aviation Experience', in G. C. Hufbauer and C. Findlay (eds.), *Flying High: Liberalizing Civil Aviation in the Asia Pacific*, Institute for International Economics, Washington, DC.

Jordan, W.A. (1970), *Airline Regulation in America: Effects and Imperfections*, Johns Hopkins University Press, Baltimore, MD.

Jordan, W.A. (1979), 'Comparisons of American and Canadian Airline Regulation', in G. B. Reschenthaler and B. Roberts (eds.) *Perspectives on Canadian Airline Regulation*, Butterworth and Co. (Canada) for the Institute for Research on Public Policy, Montreal.

Jordan, W.A. (1986), 'Results of U. S. Airline Deregulation: Evidence from the Regulated Canadian Airlines', *Logistics and Transportation Review*, vol. 22, pp. 297-337.

Joskow, P.L. and Noll, R. (1981), 'Regulation in Theory and Practice: An Overview', in G. Fromm (ed.) *Studies in Public Regulation*, MIT Press, Cambridge, MA.

Kahn, A.E. (1971), *The Economics of Regulation*, Wiley, New York.

Kanafani, A. and Keeler, T.E. (1990), 'Air Deregulation and Safety: Some Econometric Evidence', *Logistics and Transportation Review*, vol. 26, pp. 203-10.

Kane, R.M. and Vose, A.D. (1977), *Air Transportation*, 6th Edition, Kendall and Hunt, Dubuque, IA.

Keeler, T.E. (1972), 'Airline Regulation and Market Performance', *Bell Journal of Economics and Management*, vol. 3, pp. 399-414.

Keyes, L.S. (1951), 'Passenger Fare Policies of the Civil Aeronautics Board', *Journal of Air Law and Commerce*, vol. 18, pp. 25-30.

Kim, E.H. and Singal, V. (1993), 'Mergers and Market Power: Evidence from the Airline Industry', *American Economic Review*, vol. 83, pp. 549-69.

Kim, J. (1996), 'The Regulation and Growth of Civil Aviation in South Korea', in G.C. Hufbauer and C. Findlay (eds.), *Flying High: Liberalizing Civil Aviation in the Asia Pacific*, Institute for International Economics, Washington, DC.

Kim, J. (1997), 'Multiple Designation Policy in Korea', in C. Findlay, C.L. Sien and K. Singh (eds.), *Asia Pacific Air Transport: Challenges and Policy Reforms*, Institute of Southeast Asian Studies, Singapore.

Kirby, M.G. (1979), 'An Economic Assessment of Australia's Two-Airline Policy', *Australian Journal of Management*, vol. 5, pp. 105-18.

Kirby, M.G. (1981), *Domestic Airline Regulation: The Australian Study*, The Centre for Independent Study, Sydney.

Kirby, M.G. (1982), 'A Critical Examination of the Domestic Air Transport Policy Review', *Australian Economic Papers*, vol. 21, pp. 309-20.

Leahy, A.S. (1994), 'Concentration in the U.S. Airline Industry', *International Journal of Transport Economics*, vol. 21, pp. 209-15.

Lee, D.D. (1984), 'Herbert Hoover and the Development of Commercial Aviation', *Business History Review*, vol. 58, pp. 78-102.

Levine, M. (1965), 'Is Regulation Necessary? California Air Transportation and National Regulatory Policy', *Yale Law Journal*, vol. 74, pp. 1416-47.

Levine, M. (1987), 'Airline Competition in Deregulated Markets: Theory, Firm Strategy and Public Policy', *Yale Journal on Regulation*, vol. 4, pp. 393-494.

Mackinnon, J.G. (1991), 'Critical Values for Cointegration Tests', in R.F. Engle and C.W.J. Granger (eds.) *Long-Run Economic Relationships*, Oxford University Press, Oxford.

Maclay, H.K. and Burt, W.C. (1955), 'Entry of New Carriers into Domestic Trunkline Air Transportation', *Journal of Air Law and Commerce*, vol. 22, pp. 131-56.

Majone, G. (1996), 'Theories of Regulation', in G. Majone (ed.) *Regulating Europe*, Routledge, London.

May, T.E. (1986), *Independent Review of Economic Regulation of Domestic Aviation*, Australian Government Publishing Service, Canberra.

Meyer, J.R, Oster, C.V., Morgan, I.P., Berman, B.A. and Strassman, D.L. (1981), *Airline Deregulation: The Early Experience*, Auburn House, Dover, MA.

Meyer, J.R. and Strong, J.S. (1992), 'From Closed Set to Open Set Deregulation: An Assessment of the U.S. Airline Industry', *Logistics and Transportation Review*, vol. 28, pp. 1-22.

Mhatre, K. (1999a), 'Can Air-India Survive?', *Air Transport World*, vol. 36, issue 4, pp. 47-50.

Mhatre, K. (1999b), 'Sahara Girds for Growth', *Air Transport World*, vol. 36, issue 5, pp. 103-104.

Mhatre, K. (2000), 'A Decade of Turmoil', *Air Transport World*, vol. 37, issue 5, pp. 99-101.

Miller, J. R. (1981), *The Airline Deregulation Handbook*, Merton House Publishing Company, Wheaton, IL.

Minister of Transport (1984), *New Canadian Air Policy*, Transport Canada, Ottawa, May 10.

Ministry of Civil Aviation, India (2000), *The Civil Aviation Act 2000*, http://civilaviation.nic.in/ca-act/ca_act.htm.

Moore, T.G. (1986), 'U. S. Airline Deregulation Its Effects on Passengers, Capital and Labor', *Journal of Law and Economics*, vol. 29, pp. 1-28.

Morrison, S. and Winston, C.W. (1986), *The Economic Effects of Airline Deregulation*, The Brookings Institution, Washington, DC.

Morrison, S.A. and Winston, C. (1990), 'The Dynamics of Airline Pricing and Competition', *American Economic Review*, vol. 80, pp. 389-93.

Morrison, S. and Winston, C. (1995), *The Evolution of the Airline Industry*, The Brookings Institution, Washington, DC.

Morrison, S.A. and Winston, C. (1997), 'The Fare Skies: Air Transportation and Middle America', *The Brookings Review*, vol. 15, Fall, pp. 42-45.

Morrocco, J.D. (1998), 'European Commission Challenges Bilaterals', *Aviation Week and Space Technology*, March 16, p. 30.

Oster, C. and Zorn, C.K. (1989), 'Airline Deregulation: Is It Still Safe to Fly?', in L. Mosses and I. Savage (eds.) *Transportation Deregulation and Safety*, Oxford University Press, Oxford.

Oum, T. H. and Taylor, A. J. (1995), 'Emerging Patterns in Intercontinental Air Linkages and Implications for International Route Allocation Policy', *Transportation Journal*, vol. 34, pp. 5-9.

Oum, T.H. and Yu, C. (1998), *Winning Airlines*, Kluwer Academic Publishers, Norwell, MA.

Oum, T., Stanbury, W. and Tretheway, M. (1991), 'Airline Deregulation in Canada', in K. Button (ed.), *Airline Deregulation: International Experiences*, New York University Press, New York.

Peltzman, S. (1976), 'Toward a More General Theory of Regulation', *Journal of Law and Economics*, vol. 19, pp. 211-40.

Peltzman, S. (1989), 'The Economic Theory of Regulation after a Decade of Deregulation', *Brookings Papers on Microeconomics*, Special Issue, pp. 1-41.

Phillips, P. C. B. and Pierre, P. (1988), 'Time Series Regression with a Unit Root', *Biometrika*, vol. 75, pp. 335-46.

Posner, R. (1971), 'Taxation by Regulation', *Bell Journal of Economics and Management Science*, vol. 2, pp. 22-50.

Poulton, H. W. (1981), *Law, History and Politics of the Australian Two-Airline System*, H. W. Poulton, Melbourne.

Price Surveillance Authority (1992-93), *Monitoring of Movements in Average Airfares, Report*, Numbers 1-4, Melbourne.

Productivity Commission (Australia) (1997), *Economic Impact of International Airline Alliances*, Australian Government Publishing Service.

Pustay, M. (1999), 'Competition and Concentration in Canadian-U.S. Transborder Aviation Market', *Transportation Journal*, vol. 38, pp. 5-17.

Report of the Federal Aviation Commission (1935), 74th Congress, 1st Session, Senate Document No. 15.

Reynolds-Feighan, A. (2000), 'The US Airport Hierarchy and Implications for Small Communities', *Urban Studies*, vol. 37, pp. 557-77.

Richmond, S.B. (1961), *Regulation and Competition in Air Transportation*, Columbia University Press, New York.

Roller, L.R. and Sickles, R.C. (1993), 'Competition, Market Niches, and Efficiency: A Structural Model of the European Airline Industry', INSEAD Working Papers, 94/03/EPS, December.

Bibliography

Rose, N. L. (1992), 'Fear of Flying: Analyses of Airline Safety', *Journal of Economic Perspectives*, vol. 6, pp. 75-94.

Rutner, S.M., Mundy, R.A. and Whitaker, J. (1997), 'Alternatives for Reducing Delays at the United States' Busiest Airports', *Transportation Journal*, vol. 36, pp. 18-25.

Saggi, K. and Morgan, G. (1996), 'Recent Civil Aviation Experience', in G. C. Hufbauer and C. Findlay (eds.), *Flying High: Liberalizing Civil Aviation in the Asia Pacific*, Institute for International Economics, Washington, DC.

Shibata, K. (1994), 'Airline Privatization in Eastern Europe and Ex-USSR', *Logistics and Transportation Review*, vol. 30, pp. 167-88.

Shifrin, C.A. (1997), 'Northwest, Continental Shake Up Industry', *Aviation Week and Space Technology*, vol. 148, issue 5, p. 32.

Sinha, D. (1986), 'The Theory of Contestable Markets and U.S. Airline Deregulation', *Logistics and Transportation Review*, vol. 22, pp. 405-19.

Sinha, D. (1987), 'The Effects of Airline Deregulation on Airline Service from and to Nebraska', Doctoral Dissertation, University of Nebraska-Lincoln.

Sinha, D. (1993), 'Airline Regulation and Deregulation in Australia and Canada: A Comparison', *Economics*, vol. 29, no. 3, pp. 11-14.

Sinha, D. (1999), 'Evolution of Economic Regulation and Deregulation of Airlines in the USA', *Journal of Transport History*, vol. 20, 46-64.

Sinha, D. (2000), 'Airline Deregulation, Safety, Profitability and Load Factor in the United States', Mimeo.

Sinha, D. and Sinha, T. (1993), 'Australian Airline Deregulation: Grand Design or Gross Debacle?', *JASSA: Journal of the Securities Institute of Australia*, no. 3, pp. 32-33, 37.

Sinha, D. and Sinha, T. (1994a), 'Effects of Airline Deregulation: The Case of Australia', *World Competition*, vol. 17, pp. 81-96.

Sinha, T. and Sinha, D. (1994b), 'Opportunities in India: Consequences of Liberalization and Globalization', *Journal of International Marketing*, vol. 2, no. 2, pp 3-10.

Sinha, T. and Sinha, D. (1997), 'A Comparison of Development Prospects in India and China', *Asian Economies*, vol. 27, pp. 5-31.

Smithies, R. (1995), 'Air Transport and the General Agreement on Trade in Services', *Journal of Air Transport Management*, vol. 2, pp. 123-26.

Starkie, D. and Starrs, M. (1984), 'Contestability and Sustainability in Regional Airline Markets', *Economic Record*, vol. 60, pp. 274-83.

Stigler, G.J. (1971), 'The Theory of Economic Regulation', *Bell Journal of Economics and Management Science*, vol. 2, pp. 1-21.

Stigler, G.J. and Friedland, C. (1962), 'What Can Regulators Regulate? The Case of Electricity', *Journal of Law and Economics*, vol. 5, pp. 1-16.

Strassman, D. (1990), 'Potential Competition in the Deregulated Airlines', *Review of Economics and Statistics*, vol. 72, pp. 696-702.

Straszheim, M. R. (1969), *The International Airline Industry*, Washington, DC.

Taneja, N.K. (1976) *The Commercial Airline Industry*, D. C. Heath, Lexington, MA.

Taneja, N.K. (1988), The *International Airline Industry: Trends, Issues and Challenges*, D.C. Heath, Lexington, MA.

Thomas, G. (1998), 'Cutbacks Threaten Indonesian Services', *Aviation Week and Space Technology*, vol. 149, issue 3, p. 38.

Thomas, I. (2000), 'Promiscuous Alliances', *Air Transport World*, vol. 37, issue 9, pp. 35-40.

Transport Canada website (2000), http://www.tc.gc.ca/pol/en.

Trebing, H. (1987), 'Regulation of Industry: an Institutional Approach', *Journal of Economic Issues*, vol. 21, 1707-37.

Trengove, C. (1985), 'Australian Airfares', Centre of Policy Studies, Monash University, June, Working Paper.

Truitt, L. J. and Elser, M. (1996), 'Airport Privatization: Full Divestiture and its Alternatives', *Policy Studies Journal*, vol. 24, pp. 100-10.

Van Scyoc, L. (1989), 'Effects of Airline Deregulation on Profitability', *Logistics and Transportation Review*, vol. 25, pp. 39-51.

Vietor, R.H.K. (1990), 'Contrived Competition: Airline Regulation and Deregulation, 1925-1988', *Business History Review*, vol. 64, pp. 61-109.

Vietor, R.H.K. (1994), *Contrived Competition: Regulation and Deregulation in America*, Harvard University Press, Cambridge, MA.

Vowles, T. M. (2000), 'The Effect of Low Fare Air Carriers on Airfares in the US', *Journal of Transport Geography*, vol. 8, pp. 121-28.

Wettenhall, R. L. (1962), 'Australia's Two-Airline System under Review', *Australian Quarterly*, vol. 34, pp. 36-46.

White, L. J. (1979), 'Economies of Scale and the Question of 'Natural Monopoly' in the Airline Industry', *Journal of Air Law and Commerce*, vol. 46, pp. 545-73.

Windle, R. and Dresner, M. (1995), 'The Short and Long Run Effects of Entry on US Domestic Air Routes', *Transportation Journal*, vol. 35, pp. 14-25.

Bibliography

Winston, C. (1993), 'Economic Deregulation: Days of Reckoning for Microeconomists', *Journal of Economic Literature*, vol. 31, pp. 1263-89.

World Bank (2000), *World Development Indicators*, CD-ROM, World Bank, Washington, DC.

Yamauchi, H. and Ito, T. (1996), 'Air Transport Policy in Japan', in G. C. Hufbauer and C. Findlay (eds.), *Flying High: Liberalizing Civil Aviation in the Asia Pacific*, Institute for International Economics, Washington, DC.

Yamauchi, H. (1997), 'Air Transport Policy in Japan: Limited Competition under Regulation', in C. Findlay, C.L. Sien and K. Singh (eds.), *Asia Pacific Air Transport: Challenges and Policy Reforms*, Institute of Southeast Asian Studies, Singapore.

Zerbe Jr., R.O. and Urban, N. (1988) 'Including the Public Interest in Theories of Regulation', in R.O. Zerbe (ed.) *Research in Law and Economics*, vol. 11, Jai Press, Greenwich, CT.

Index

Adrangi, B. 143
Air Canada, 6, 53, 57, 60-62, 66
Air Commerce Act, 87
Air Corporations Act, 15-16
Air France, 67, 70
Air India, 6, 14-16, 18-19
Air Mail Act of 1930, 88
Air Mail Act of 1934, 88
Air New Zealand, 6, 50-51
Air Services Agreement, 61
Air Transport Association, 3-4, 124-125, 142-143, 145
Air Transport Board, 56-57
air transport liberalisation packages, 73
Airline Agreement (Termination) Act of 1990, 34
Airline Deregulation Act, 1, 39, 49, 69, 71-72, 77, 91, 101-102, 106, 126, 129, 145
Airline Industry Investigation, 94
Airlines Agreement Act, 36
Airmail Act, 86-87
Alamdari, F.E. 4, 75
Al-Jazzaf, M. 6
All Nippon Airways, 24
American Airlines, 8, 10, 62, 70, 88, 94, 96, 99
Ansett, 7, 36-44, 48, 50-51
Armstrong, M. 82
Asiana Airlines, 30
asymmetric information, 82-83
Australian Airlines, 7, 35-40, 42, 50

Australian Competition and Consumer Commission, 44
average length of haul, 69
Averch, H. 84
Averch-Johnson theory, 84

Bailey, E.E. 4, 98-99, 104-105, 109-111, 119, 126
Bain, J.S. 112
Baldwin, J.R. 56
Banerjee, A. 141
Bangkok Airways, 31
Barrett, S.D. 68, 75-76
Bates, G.L. 95
Baumol, W.J. 46, 103, 112-113, 119-120
Becker, G. 85
Berge, S. 93, 95
Berry, S.T. 124
Borenstein, S. 124-125, 140-141
break-even load factor, 3, 32
Brenner, M.A. 137
Breyer, S.G. 99, 102
Briand, S. 67
British Airways, 2, 6, 8, 50, 67, 70, 74
Brogden, S. 34-35
Bureau of Transport and Communications Economics, 46, 48-49
Bureau of Transport Economics, 38-39, 41, 44-45, 47
Burt, W.C. 96

Butler, R.V. 131
Button, K. 69, 76-77

Cabotage, 4-5, 73, 135
Canadian Airlines, 53, 55, 57, 60-62
Captain, P.F. 73
Card, D. 135-136
Caves, D.W. 39, 99, 125
Caves, R.E. 84, 87-88, 94, 96
Chicago Convention, 4, 20, 35, 68-
   70, 134
Chow, G. 143
Christensen, L.R. 39, 99, 125
Civil Aeronautics Act, 80, 91-93, 96,
   102
Civil Aeronautics Board, 80-81, 91,
   94-95, 97, 99
Civil Aviation Agreement Act 1957,
   36
Civil Aviation Authority, 20, 74-75
Clinton, O.V. 137
code-sharing, 7, 19, 61
cointegration tests, 144
Commission of the European
   Communities, 77
Common Transport Policy, 68
Compass, 7, 42-49
contestability theory, 46-47, 75, 109-
   110, 112, 119
contestable market, 46, 103
Cowan, S. 82
Crane, J.B. 96
Cunningham, L.J. 49

Davies, G.D. 37-38
Demsetz, H. 85
Department of Economic Affairs,
   17-19
Department of Transport, 34, 38, 42,
   56
Department of Transport and
   Communications, 34, 42

Department of Transportation, 97,
   101, 123-124, 126, 128-129, 131-
   132
discount airfares, 44-45
Domestic Passenger Fare
   Investigation, 97, 106
Douglas, E.J. 49
Douglas, G.W. 98, 107
Dresner, M. 127

Eads, G. 99
economic theory of regulation, 81,
   84-85
economies of density, 39, 99, 125-
   126
economies of scale, 39, 104-105,
   116, 119, 125
economies of vehicle scale, 39
Essential Air Service Act, 78
excessive competition, 80, 88, 90, 93
externalities, 83

Federal Airport Act, 94
Federal Aviation Act of 1958, 96
Feldman, J.M. 10
Fifth Freedom, 4
Findlay, C. 51-52
First Freedom, 4
Flint, P. 61
Forsyth, P. 38-39
Fourth Freedom, 4
frequent flier programs, 7, 45, 120,
   121, 140-141
Friedland, C. 84
Fueille, P. 135

Gallaghar, T. 20-21
Garuda, 22-23
General Agreement on Trade in
   Services, 10
Gill, F.W. 95
Goldberg, S. 55

Gomez-Ibanez, J.A. 137
Good, D.H. 5, 69, 76
Goodman, W.C. 138-139
Gourdin, K.N. 9, 134
Graham, B. 70-73, 75
Graham, D. R. 4, 39, 98-99, 105,
    108-110, 119, 126
grandfather clause, 92
grandfather rights, 68
Granger causality tests, 143, 147
Green, H. 41

Haddon-Cave, C.P. 34
Harberger, A. 81
Hendricks, W. 135-136
Herfindahl index, 106-107, 111, 118,
    122, 127
Hirsch, B.T. 136
Hocking, C.P. 34
Hocking, R.D. 38-39
Holcroft, W. 37-38
hub airports, 68, 71, 124, 132
hub and spoke operations, 50, 60,
    123, 133
hub and spoke system, 18, 70, 124-
    126, 139
Humphreys, B. 74, 76
Hurdle, G.J. 115, 117, 129
Huston, J.H. 131

Independent Air Fares Committee
    Act, 37
Indian Airlines, 14-19
institutional theory of regulation, 83-
    84
intermodal competition, 49-50, 70
Interstate Commerce Commission,
    81, 89--91
Ito, T. 24, 26

Jaggi, G. 51
Japan Air System, 24
Japan Airlines, 6, 10, 24, 26

Jenkins, D. 20-21
Johnson, K. 69, 77
Johnson, L. 84
Jordan, W.A. 57-59, 98, 102, 134
Joskow, P.L. 84, 117

Kahn, A.E. 98-99
Kaldor-Hicks test, 81
Kanafani, A. 142
Kane, R.M. 88
Kaplan, D.P. 4, 39, 98-99, 108-111,
    119, 126
Keeler, T.E. 98, 142
Kelkar Committee, 16
Kelvin, A. 67
Keyes, L.S. 95
Kim, E.H. 126
Kim, J. 30-31
Kirby, M.G. 38, 41
Kissling, C. 51
KLM, 6, 8-9, 29
Korean Airlines, 30
Korean National Airlines, 30

Labour costs, 4, 75
large hubs, 121-122, 131
Leahy, A.S. 126
Lee, D.D. 86
Leet, J.O. 137
Levine, M. 98, 140-141
Likely Potential Entrants, 115-117
load factor, 3-4, 22-23, 32, 36, 38-
    39, 43, 64-65, 74, 97, 100, 102,
    106, 107-109, 116-118, 122, 125,
    139, 143, 145-147
Lufthansa, 2, 6, 9-10, 23, 67

Mackinnon, J.G. 146
Maclay, H.K. 96
Macpherson, D.A. 136
Majone, G. 83
Malaysian Airlines, 6-7, 28-29
May, T.E. 38-39

medium hubs, 106, 121-123
Meyer, J.R. 100, 138
Mhatre, K. 14-15, 18-19
Miller III, J.C. 98, 107
Miller, J.R. 101
minimum efficient scale, 39, 115
Minister of Transport, 26, 58, 62
Ministry of Civil Aviation, India, 15,
    18-19, 20
Moore, T.G. 112, 114
Morgan, G. 31, 51
Morrell, P. 4, 75
Morrison, S. 75, 112-113, 115, 119,
    121-124, 140
Morrocco, J.D. 135
Mundy, R.A. 133, 148

Natural monopoly, 83, 99, 115
Navigation Act of 1920, 34-35, 47
Nerlove, M. 99
Noll, R. 84
nonhubs, 106, 121-123, 125

Oster, C. 141
Oum, T. 8, 28, 58-59
overbooking, 3

Panzar, J.C. 46, 103-105, 112, 119
Pareto optimality, 103
"Peanuts" fares, 99
Peltzman, S. 85
Perron, P. 145-146
Phillips, P.C.B. 145-146
Pickrell, D.H. 137
place utility, 2
Posner, R. 85
Poulton, H.W. 34-35
Price Surveillance Authority, 42-44
productivity, 4, 21, 41, 59, 63, 68,
    75-76, 96, 138-139
Productivity Commission, 8
public interest theory of regulation,
    81-83

Pustay, M. 58

Qantas, 6, 7, 29, 42, 44, 50-51

Raduchel, W. 99
Raffiee, K. 143
*Report of the Federal Aviation
    Commission*, 90-91, 93
Reynolds-Feighan, A. 122, 129-131
Richmond, S.B. 91
Roller, L.R. 5, 69, 72, 76
Rose, N.L. 141
Rutner, S.M. 133, 148

Safety, 20, 30, 39-40, 52, 59-60, 74,
    86-89, 91, 96-98, 100, 120, 142-
    147
Saggi, K. 31
Schott, E. 137
Second Freedom, 4
Seventh Freedom, 5
Shibata, K. 78
Shifrin, C.A. 9
Sibley, D.S. 105, 108-109, 111, 119
Sickles, R.C. 5, 69, 72-73, 76
Singal, V. 126
Singapore Airlines, 6-7, 17, 28, 51
Sinha, D. 13, 15, 42, 46, 48, 59, 113-
    114, 121, 143, 146-147
Sinha, T. 13, 15, 42, 48
Sixth Freedom, 5, 74
small hubs, 106, 121-123
Smithies, R. 11
Stanbury, W. 59
Starkie, D. 46
Starrs, M. 46
Stein, L.R. 102
Stigler, G.J. 84-85
Strassman, D. 127
Straszheim, M.R. 99
Strong, J.S. 138
Summers, L. 141
'Supersaver' fares, 99

Swissair, 8, 10, 29
Szerezen, C. 135

Taneja, N.K. 12, 72, 77, 85-87, 96
Taylor, A.J. 8
Thai Airways, 6-7, 31
The National Transportation Act, 57-
58
theories of regulation, 71, 81, 121
Third Freedom, 4
Thomas, G. 22, 51
time utility, 2
transborder passengers, 60, 66
Transport Act of 1938, 56
Transport Canada, 54, 61-65
Trebing, H. 83
Trengrove, C. 40
Tretheway, M. 39, 59, 99, 125

United Airlines, 7, 61, 70, 96
Urban, N. 81-82

Van Scyoc, L. 137
Vickers, J. 82
Vietor, R.H.K. 85, 100
Voss, A.D. 88
Vowles, T.M. 128

Wettenhall, R.L. 38
Whitaker, J. 133, 148
Willig, R.D. 46, 103, 112-113, 129
Windle, R. 127
Winston, C. 75, 112-113, 119, 121-
124, 136, 140
World Bank, 14, 22, 25, 28, 30, 32,
68

Yamauchi, H. 24, 26-28
yield, 3-4, 13, 40, 45, 49, 59, 61,
109, 111, 115-118, 127, 137
Yu, C. 28, 58

Zerbe Jr., R.O. 81-82
Zorn, C.K. 141